VITA CARMELITANA

or

LIFE IN CARMEL

Translated by
REV. LEO J. WALTER, *O. CARM.*

1934

APPROBATION

"VITA CARMELITANA" is an excellent and authentic exposition of the character and spirit of the Carmelite life and may well serve as the official text-book on this subject.

To bring its doctrine within easy reach of all the members of our Province this translation from the original Latin text was made.

We give the book in its present form the approbation it merits and urge the perusal of its pages upon all,—novice and veteran alike.

September 2, 1934.

FR. LAWRENCE C. DIETHER, *O. Carm.*
Provincial.

Nihil Obstat

JOHN B. FURAY, S. J.
Censor Deputatus

October 10, 1934,

Imprimatur

GEORGE CARDINAL MUNDELEIN, D.D.
Archbishop of Chicago

October 30, 1934.

FATHER GENERAL'S LETTER
TO SUPERIORS

In October, 1932, the novice-masters of the Order were summoned to Rome to consider the education of our young men. From this meeting we have derived many advantages. Gathered together, they form this booklet which we have been long anxious to send to you.

Consequently it is our wish and command that you studiously, carefully and thoroughly read this book so that the principles it contains may be put into daily practice as expeditiously and as becomingly as such matter demands. Should you practice them, you will obtain great advantage for your soul, and will become expert in virtue. By you and through you the enthusiasm of the rest of the brethren will be enkindled and the whole Order of Carmel will at last be afire with zeal for virtue.

If you are animated with love for God and the Blessed Virgin Mary of Mount Carmel, apply every stirring of your mind and heart, and every effort of your being to attain this ideal of perfection.

Hereby we admonish and we warn all Superiors, whether major or local, to take measures to have the teachings of this book applied in the training of our youth, so that their souls may the more readily be conformed to the "Life In Carmel," lest even one of them whom God has joined to us, stray away and perish.

Such is our wish, such our command. It is your duty to obey this command.

Given at Rome from our College of St. Albert, May 10, 1933.

HILARY J. DOSWALD,
Prior General .

INDEX

PREFACE

IN OCTOBER, 1932, the novice-masters of the Carmelite Order held a convention in Rome for the purpose of establishing uniformity in the training of novices. Almost a year before, the subjects of papers were assigned to those judged to be best qualified to discuss them. This fact alone is proof of the importance attached to the meeting by the superiors of the Order and is a guarantee of the soundness of the doctrine presented. To satisfy a widely expressed desire the conclusions were published by order of the Most Rev. Father General. However, the papers were not published as read; to avoid digressions and repetitions which under the circumstances were inevitable, a synthesis was made of the important conclusions and published under the title "Vita Carmelitana." As the book in Latin would have only a limited usefulness, a translation has been made into English which is hereby given.

The sources of quotations are not indicated, as they are readily available in the original to those who are interested.

A word of explanation from the Latin Preface will not be out of place.

"Some may wonder why our old Constitutions of the Reform of Tours, as it is called, are so frequently quoted. A reason will be given at once.

"In the first place these Constitutions are undoubtedly the chief foundation of our present Constitutions. This will be patent by only a brief comparison. Therefore our present Constitutions cannot be better explained than by reference to the others.

"Secondly, the ascetical teaching of Carmel is nowhere more profoundly and clearly explained and established. De facto all introductions placed at the head of the various chapters of our Constitutions in which some spiritual advice or the general principles of religious life are stated, have from the beginning been found in the Constitutions of that Reform. Nor is there anyone who will deny that they are very beautiful and profound. We know moreover that they were not composed at haphazard by men of mean authority and experience, but rather that they were composed with fasting and prayer by holy men who were striving with fervor and love to restore the Order in the true spirit of Carmel and who were by no means ignorant of the secrets of higher contemplation.

"Finally this Reform was begun not on the private authority of an individual religious, but by the authority and the command of Father Henry Silvius, the Prior General of the whole Order. Ventimiglia gives the following testimony:—In Gaul he sowed the first seeds of the Reformation and the strict observance of the Province of Tours. This Reform by means of the Constitutions made for it and afterward approved by Urban VIII (1630), and again enlarged and confirmed by Innocent X (1646), grew to such an extent that to his great credit it was also extended to other Provinces. Moreover, Innocent ordered that these Constitutions should be observed inviolably in all the reformed Provinces."

Thus they were in use in the Province of Syracuse in Sicily, called "S. Mariae de Scala: Paradisi," and they have been introduced together with the Reform into a great part of the Order. It is evident we are not drawing from foreign sources.

PART I

In What the Truly Carmelite Life Consists

CHAPTER I

*How important it is to know and to follow the spirit of
one's Order.*

WE shall hardly know how to train our novices,
unless we are thoroughly acquainted with our
aim. Wherefore, the novice-master should before all
things, know the aim and manner of Carmelite life.
Every novice-master worthy of the name must first of
all ask himself after what pattern he shall mould the
character of his novices. For the novice-master who
has not sketched for himself the image of a true and
perfect Carmelite, is like an architect trying to erect
a building without knowing what style of building to
follow. Without doubt, such a one acts rashly. He
may, perhaps, turn out novices remarkable for piety,
without imbuing them with the spirit of his Order.
For the means are determined by the end.

In this matter two dangers must be avoided. First
we must not stress our specialties at the expense of
those features common to all Orders or even to all
men striving for perfection; secondly, we must not
frame a false idea of a truly Carmelite life.

In order to avoid the former danger we must be
convinced that the common foundation of religious
life cannot be destroyed with impunity. All of us
fundamentally are called to one and the same and
which is to glorify God, to propagate his kingdom
among men according to our means and so to make
ourselves holy and perfect, or as our Rule says, to live
in the following of Christ."

The perfection for which each and every religious is bound to strive by his very profession is not a different one in each Order; in fact, one and the same perfection is set before religious and seculars. All spiritual writers agree that it consists in perfect charity. Consequently, the essential means to attain perfection cannot differ in the various Orders. For no one can be said to be perfect or established in charity unless he has renounced sin, has plucked out the roots of evil and vice, and has acquired the virtues. For all of which, we stand in need not only of divine grace, but also of the means to procure grace and of self-abnegation by which to attain grace and to prevent grace from losing its effect before the assaults of nature and of the passions.

It is not prudent to despise those counsels which others from the teaching of experience and on account of the very nature of religious life follow with so much fruit. We may not spurn them led by the sole motive that they are championed by the writers of other Orders, unless they are opposed to our manner of life. "Prove all things; hold fast to that which is good."

Likewise we may not reject certain means of perfection which have been taught and approved for centuries, merely because they seem to have been unknown to our forefathers, e.g., the particular examen, methodical prayer and meditation at appointed times, etc., particularly since ordinarily we do not follow the fathers to the letter, and what is more we cannot follow them so. Whatever benefits us and does not force us to forsake the truly Carmelite life and the spirit of our fathers, we should gladly adopt without envy and without rivalry so that God may be honored and the kingdom of God be spread. For the same spirit worketh in all.

By no means must we think that belittling and depreciating others will be an advantage to our

Order or to our spiritual life. Pride, vain glory, envy, false rivalry are hateful and harmful in individuals and in a community. All Orders are members of the Church and of her mystic body, and draw their life from the same source. All are created by Divine Providence for this same end, that under the guidance of the Church, they may procure God's glory and the salvation of souls. With good reason our Constitutions warn us: "Let our religious everywhere shun boasting of themselves and too great exaggeration about our affairs. They should always speak in praise of other Orders and if they should hear anything unfavorable about them, they should modestly and simply excuse it."

The whole question is very clearly explained in these words to which we cannot help giving our assent. "Certainly all the essentials of the spiritual life are found in every truly Catholic school of spirituality, drawn as it is from the very Gospel. But the proportion among these elements, the manner of uniting and adapting them, so that one body of doctrine and life should spring from them, is not the same in all the schools."

Standard means must not be despised nor characteristic ones slighted. If one by his vocation belongs to a certain school of spirituality it is harmful to embrace another school or to mix the elements from several schools. That is why our manner of life should be adopted and practiced with singular affection by all true Carmelites. To this life we are called; for it we receive necessary graces; by this life we shall arrive at perfection.

The Venerable Michael of St. Augustine says: "Since our Rule is so well organized and adapted to our purpose, there is no reason why we should look elsewhere or beg from other sources the means to attain the desired perfection."

[9]

It is not proper to forsake the spirit of one's own Order in order to imitate other Orders. The Order will reap much harm, not merely if a few religious do so, but more so if the Order is unfaithful to itself and departs from the footsteps of its fathers, greedy of novelties and vainglory, and seduced by an unholy rivalry. It will never reap more and richer fruits for itself and for the whole kingdom of God, than when it strives to respond faithfully to God's intention and will in its regard. It will never make progress, until it has conformed itself to its proper genius and character. Other Orders hold their place in the Church of God with great fruit in other ways, but he who continually sways to and fro along several paths, will always be excelled by the others.

Then there is a second danger, as we stated above, of proposing to ourselves a wrong idea of genuine Carmelite life, unconsciously allowing ourselves to be influenced by our own whims or those of others. The master of novices must especially be on his guard not to set before the novices a standard drawn from Religious who observe their rules badly, or from his own defects, or from customs illegally introduced into the community. For the novices have the sacred right to have the ideal of the true and genuine Carmelite set before them.

The uncontaminated sources to draw from will be:—

1—Our Holy Rule which is the fundamental and permanent law which may not be adulterated. If we depart from our Rule, we lose the true spirit of Carmel.

2—Our Constitutions which are, as it were, an appendix to the Rule. They are certain sparks of the divine law, from which they derive force and power for the observance of the vows according to the Rule. They may not be considered mere counsels.

They are the bonds of cloistral discipline, repeatedly strengthened in our Order so that the Order itself may be more firmly established. Although our primitive Rule of St. Albert was in days gone by sufficient for our forefathers entirely given to contemplation in solitude, the change of our state and the addition of the care of souls have compelled the Rule to be supplemented and perfected by new decrees.

It is the scope of the Constitutions to defend and preserve the spirit of the Rule in these changed circumstances and times. They must, therefore, be interpreted in such a way as not to contradict the Rule.

3—Our traditions lasting for centuries, of which the following are witnesses:—

> a—The book called "De institutione primorum monachorum in Lege veteri exortoruin et in nova perseverantium." This book is called the Rule of John 44 in which the strictly solitary and contemplative life is highly praised and which even after the Rule of St. Albert, has remained in use amongst us as an ascetical treatise.

> It will not be out of place to add here a letter written by Nicholas of Gaul, which attempts to protect the strictly solitary and contemplative life against every corruption. Venerable John of St. Samson explicitly appeals to this book.

> b—Official Documents, i.e., Decrees of General Chapters, Ancient Constitutions, Reports of Visitations, Letters of the Priors General, etc.

> c—Authors of our Order.

What do we find in these sources?

Our Rule tells us, "Let each one remain in his cell meditating day and night on the law of the Lord, and watching in prayer unless occupied in other just employment." Here, uninterrupted conversation with God, continuous meditation on divine things, in one word, contemplation is enjoined upon us Carmelites. Toward this Carmelites must always aspire and have no care for other things except they are necessary for life. Consequently the assiduous labor to which we are advised by Chapter XV has no other aim than "that the devil may find us occupied lest on account of our idleness he may be able to find an avenue of approach to our souls." According to the mind of the legislator purity of mind, and therefore contemplation, is safeguarded by assiduous labor.

In agreement with this teaching are the words of the author of "De institutione primorum monachorum." "The aim of this life is discovered to be twofold. The first we attain by our effort and by the practice of virtue assisted by divine grace. This means to offer God a perfect heart, free from the dross of actual sin. The second aim of this life is realized solely by a gift of God, namely, to taste with the heart and to experience in the mind in some measure at least, not merely after death, but in this mortal life, the power of God's presence and the intoxication of supernal glory." It is evident to all that there is question here not of two co-ordinated ends, but of one subordinated to the other. Let us notice also that our author proposes to us Carmelites, the highest contemplation, the mystical experience as it is called, or infused contemplation, as his words themselves clearly indicate.

Even though this Rule of John 44 refers directly to the times before the Rule of St. Albert, still even after the migration of the Carmelites to Europe, it continued to be held in high esteem, since it seemed to our ancestors to express the true Carmelite spirit which it was their duty to preserve and to cultivate in their changed circumstances. Indeed the General

Chapter held in Montpellier in 1287 says, "We recognize that we have left the world in order to enable ourselves to converse familiarly with God." The Constitutions of 1324 say, "The holy fathers both of the New and Old Testament were lovers of solitude in Carmel for the sake of contemplating heavenly things. Without doubt they made their dwelling near the fountain of Elias for the sake of penance which they practiced without ceasing."

All our writers defend this same spirit and our Constitutions especially since the Reform of Tours, as it is called, have striven to safeguard it.

We may omit St. Theresa and the Mystic Doctor, St. John of the Cross. How greatly he desired to restore the purely contemplative life is known to all. We shall recall the authors of our Observance among whom are eminent that famous mystic, the blind Brother John of St. Samson, and Father Michael of St. Augustine. That Brother John of St. Samson was not only endowed with the gift of highest contemplation but also that he endeavored by all means to enkindle all Carmelites with an intense love of prayer, is evident from all his writings.

From Father Michael of St. Augustine we shall quote only these words:—"Our venerable and learned Thomas of Waldo had well considered when he wrote, 'Now let St. Dominic appear in his heavenly doctrine; then St. Francis in renunciation and contempt of the world; then let our lawgiver, Albert, appear with the dwellers on Carmel and let them progress in silence, in the solitude of their cells, and in assiduous prayer in the law of the Lord.' As though this pious and learned Father would say, 'Let the religious of other Orders glory in their respective aims; but let a Carmelite glory in his vocation which is to meditate day and night on the law of the Lord and to have unceasing conversation with God in watchfulness and prayer.' "

CHAPTER II

The Contemplative Life

Prayer

HOW IS THE Carmelite life to be organized? To this question we say, "All those things must be observed without which a life of prayer and contemplation cannot flourish. For this reason we must pay special attention to prayer and contemplation itself."

It will, therefore, be necessary to apply oneself at fixed times to prayer and contemplation exclusively, so that we may really treat with God alone in the strict sense of the word. This follows necessarily from the fact that we are now called to the public service of the Church and to cultivate the vineyard of the Lord. Whereas, since practically only one thing was necessary to our Carmelite forefathers hidden in their anchorages and caves, viz., to treat with God by means of contemplation, that one precept of the Rule about abiding in the cells and continuous meditation and contemplation was sufficient. "Other just employments," especially outside the cells, seem to have been rather few. They did not stand in need of appointed hours for making meditation, since nearly all their time was taken up in meditating. Now, however, since "other just employments" arrogate to themselves the greater part of the day, I am inclined to think the contemplative life itself would be in danger, if certain hours were not dedicated to the exercises of piety. If all things were left to the judgment of the individual it surely would come to such a pass that religious, especially the younger ones, would neglect prayer, and deceived by false reasons, would give themselves over entirely to external employments or even to sloth. At least the Order itself would be no help to the religious, because the religious of goodwill would frequently be hindered from conversing with God by these others.

Besides not one of us appears to have even a doubt in the matter. It is the common opinion prevalent among us and no one has ever taught otherwise, since it is clearly and openly affirmed in the Constitutions themselves. In explaining the nature of our Order, they call the contemplative life the foundation and chief characteristic of our Order, "fundamentum et partem principaliorem."

The pursuit of divine contemplation and the love of holy solitude are said to have been formerly the only, but are now the chief, portion of our Order. And "in order that this spirit or the primitive purpose of our holy Order may flourish always amongst us, one eremitical convent is to be established in those Provinces in which it can be done."

The Constitutions, therefore, desire and also provide that the contemplative spirit should not weaken and die. Moreover, they inculcate that according to the primitive prophetical institute of the Patriarch Elias, Carmelites are principally called to sing the divine praises. They establish as a principle, and it is their desire to impress it at once and deeply upon our minds, that prayer is the life of a religious. Should prayer weaken, life will weaken; should prayer flourish, life will be vigorous too. And they continue, "This is so true in our Order that we profess its first and chief aim to be found in prayer and contemplation."

Again, when they have occasion to recommend the study of literature and science, they do not hesitate to affirm that mystical theology is without doubt the best portion of Carmelites.

We may point out here that they do not merely say that contemplation is the foundation of Carmelite life, but also its chief aim, "partem principaliorem." The contemplative life seems to be the foundation for all mixed Orders, as they are called, or such as are called to the apostolate. For according to St. Thomas and other authors zeal for souls must spring from contemplation, so that a true and successful apostolate cannot be exercised without it. But for us Carmelites the contemplative life which in itself is said to excel the active life, is not demanded because of the apostolate, nor is it in itself organized for the apostolate, but for us Carmelites contemplation is our vocation. Thus, every true Carmelite will before all things and according to his best power summon every effort to become perfect in it. A certain novice-master was wont to say, "Our Constitutions, as is fitting, and our Rule put the essence of our Order in the mixed life, not in the mixed life simply as such, but as for one in greater part and principally contemplative, i.e., they put the essence of our Order in prayer and contemplation as its foundation and chief characteristic."

Carmelites, therefore, in obedience to their Rule, should strive to be solely occupied with God unless detained in exterior occupations for higher motives, just as the magnetic needle always points north unless deflected by force. The Order itself should lead the way to this end, so that its religious may before all things acquire the art of mental prayer and persevere in its exercise with great fervor. Unless the Order does so, it seems to be a traitor to itself and to relinquish its right to its chief and best inheritance-all with great loss to itself and to its members.

Yes, the Order would show itself a mother unfaithful to her children, were she to deny them that very thing which they rightfully and before all things demand. Here the words of the Prophet come to mind, "The little ones have asked for bread, and there was none to break it unto them." In fact, it would look as though stones instead of bread, were being given them.

In view of all this, we naturally ask ourselves how life on Carmel is to be organized in order that the chief feature be not weakened or lost. What conclusions of a practical nature can be drawn from the principle now evident?

With good reason, therefore, the rule of making meditation at fixed times was introduced into our Order, as into all other Orders, after the XVI century.

SECTION ONE

Meditation

THE GENERAL CHAPTER of 1593 held at Cremona in which the Discalced Carmelites were allowed to separate from us says, "Since man approaches more closely to God in proportion as he is despoiled of human acts, and since contemplation and mental prayer join men to God, we wish our religious to practice this holy meditation, and we ordain that this sacred tribute be paid to God twice a day, in the morning after Prime and in the evening after the ringing of the Angelus. When the signal has been given, all without exception, shall go to the choir and give themselves for a half hour to mental prayer and contemplation."

Meditation is prescribed in the decrees published for the Province of Spain and Portugal in 1595, and in the Constitutions of the Congregation of Mantua published in 1602. The Reform of Tours, as it is called, orders two meditations of an hour each to be made every day. Thus it followed the example of Fr. Philip Thibault, the chief promoter of the Reform, who even before he was bound by any law as to the duration of meditation, impelled only by the desire of progressing in the way of God, spent every day two hours, or at least one and a half hour, in this angelic exercise. He did this even when he was most occupied in teaching the higher sciences or engaged in preaching lenten courses.

Though the Constitutions of 1637 speak of a half hour's meditation twice a day, those printed shortly afterward again prescribe two meditations, and then continue, "Meditation shall be made thus. In the morning at 5:30 the Angelus will ring and will also be the signal for meditation. Everyone without exception, viz., officials, preachers, confessors and the rest of the clerics will proceed to the place designated by the Prior. Each one will spend an hour on matter prepared privately according to the form of prayer outlined in our Directories. Similarly the evening meditation will begin after Vespers; in lent after Complin. But this will last only a half hour." In houses of study the morning meditation lasted only a half hour.

Today, however, as all know, we are obliged by art. 149 of our Constitutions to mental prayer which as far as possible should be one hour a day. It is the wish of the General Chapter held in 1931, that the morning meditation last an hour even if then the evening meditation be omitted.

This demand, without doubt, is slight when compared with the prescriptions of the Rule. For this reason it should be so much more carefully observed, unless we wish to have our contemplative life and our chief and best heritage reduced to nothing. This would be a disgrace to us Carmelites, particularly in these times when so many of the faithful living in the world consecrate much time to prayer and meditation. With best reason, therefore, do our Constitutions not only command that those who cannot be at meditation with the Community make it privately, but also forbid that anyone be called from meditation, without urgent reason when all make it in common.

Therefore, Superiors do wrong when they easily dispense or when they hinder mental prayer by an abundance of vocal prayers or by devotions that are not prescribed. Likewise religious do wrong when they try to escape meditation for trivial reasons or consider any occupation preferable to mental prayer. Our saints acted differently. We read about the Ven. Angelus Paoli in the Acts of his Beatification: He was never absent from the meditations prescribed by the Rule. Content with the least possible sleep he would pass whole nights in the contemplation of heavenly things. When he was told, as often happened, that he was in need of longer rest because of the worn-out condition of his body, he would answer that to one in love with God no sweeter rest could come than that of St. John,—rest, i.e., prayer on the breast of Christ. Often during the day he hid himself in retired places in order to refresh his spirit for several hours in prayer, which to him meant the effort to bring God to himself. In the same way he prepared himself very diligently for Holy Mass which he celebrated with fervor of heart. After the celebration of the Mass he would practice such recollection that he would listen to no one, and tend to no business, considering it a sin to be drawn aside after tasting the sacred Host and to talk about other things than God. No one, however, will accuse our Venerable brother of neglecting either the corporal or spiritual necessities of his neighbor on account of excessive contemplation.

Fr. Michael of St. Augustine, according to the testimony of Fr. Timothy of the Presentation, was not only the first to hasten to choir but also the last to leave, always remaining long after the others in prayer and meditation, and always in such a position of body that there seemed to be only one difference betweeen him and a dead man: occasionally, owing to chronic hoarseness, he had to cough. Furthermore he was so strongly addicted to the practice of contemplation that he would dedicate, if not the entire night, at least half the night to it. Even when he had made a journey of miles on foot, he was usually seen to rise from his bed right after Matins at midnight and go to the choir in order to pour out his heart in sweetness of prayer before his hidden God.

Concerning the prayer of Fr. Michael de la Fuente we can affirm that in as far as it was humanly possible, his prayer was not only perpetual, but his very life and soul. Frequently after giving the whole day to preaching, to hearing confessions, to reconciling enemies, and to similar apostolic labors which he performed throughout that region, he would give himself tired as he was to prayer and contemplation for the entire night, or surely the greater part of the night.

These men, burning as they were with apostolic zeal, conversed with God more than other men and no one can doubt that they drew from meditation and contemplation so efficacious a love and zeal for souls. How seriously, therefore, do they err and offend not only against the Order, but also against the salvation of souls, who think that the chief feature of Carmelite life should be reduced to a minimum on account of apostolic work! So it will happen that the interior spirit of the Order will die, and the external work will be without fruit. Those who despise prayer, often without knowing, destroy what has been accomplished with great fervor and exertion; and when the foundation of divine grace has been spurned, the whole edifice in all its splendor, but built by merely human hands, quickly collapses. Wherefore the Ven. Angelus Paoli used to say that preachers of the Gospel work more by prayer and example than by study and words; and for this reason he especially recommended to them the practice of prayer.

What has been said is confirmed by John Baptist Rossi of Ravenna, the celebrated Prior General and contemporary of St. Theresa, who in 1568 published a compendium of the Constitutions for the Italian Provinces:—The chief and foremost endeavors of those first dwellers on Mount Carmel, (and this, those who profess the Carmelite life now must imitate and embrace), were directed toward using every effort day and night to join their heart and soul to God the Father in prayer, contemplation and uninterrupted love, not merely habitually but actually.

SECTION TWO

The Divine Office

BESIDES mental prayer, whether meditation or contemplation, vocal prayer is necessary to the contemplative life, because it is not possible that the mind be always occupied in pure contemplation, and moreover mental prayer of its own nature leads to vocal prayer. For this reason the eighth chapter of our Rule prescribes that those who know how to say the canonical hours with the clerics should say them according to the regulations of the holy Fathers and the approved custom of the church. Inspired by these words our Constitutions ordain that "as soon as the signal for the day or night hours has been sounded, the Brethren should prepare themselves and at the appointed hour quickly assemble to go into the church; there, humbly and devoutly to discharge the divine offices." Going beyond the Canon Law, they urge that the Office be recited in choir "even when four are not present."

What has been said about making mental prayer at fixed hours holds also of the Divine Office. In olden days the Constitutions demanded that the Brethren rise at night not merely to recite but to sing Matins in the oratory. Surely we should with great diligence and perseverance accomplish what remains, and in this way we can in union with the Church exercise the apostolate of prayer as it is called.

The Constitutions clearly inculcate the following: "No one under pretext of any privilege whatsoever should be considered exempt from choir except for the time in which he is actually occupied in the discharge of his office; moreover such time should be prudently and in conscience limited by the Superiors."

Here it may not be amiss to remember a prohibition of the year 1593: "It is not lawful for the Prior to grant permission for going out of the monastery during the time of Office, except for urgent business, or for a public need which does not bear delay, and is known to the Prior; anyone having obtained such a permission must return at the proper time in order to be present at Mass and the Hours."

Carmelites are called not only to make private meditation, but also to chant the praises of God with others. By the recitation of the Divine Office a contemplative guards against narrowing himself down to his own notions and against being completely wrapped up in himself, forgetful of others and the common good of the Church. For the recitation of the Divine Office, particularly such as is done in choir, is an active communion with the mystical body of Christ. Therefore it is to be preferred to any and every private prayer. Chanting the Office, provided it is properly done, that is, "digne, attente ac devote," does not only not hinder meditation and contemplation, but helps much, particularly if we will observe those points which the Ven. John of St. Samson counsels: "Before you begin your canonical hours, ask God for complete and perfect attention, protesting that you neither wish nor desire anything else than his honor and glory. Renounce all distractions, imaginations, anxieties. Do this as perfectly as possible and with the greatest love, the while despising them and considering them less than nothing." Provided we apply our soul and our spirit to God during vocal prayer as much as we can, it matters not whether we have the literal sense of the word or not, unless it should be perfectly clear of itself. For then we must accept it as given and infused by God and for some time we must allow ourselves to be inflamed by the love of God without our ceasing to follow the Office." And again! "To know rather than to love, is to be united and attached more to oneself than to God." Finally, "When you say Office, it is not necessary to seek the entire sense, but to apply your mind to it only insofar as it offers itself to you. In that case you are compelled toward it, as it were, by a sharp goad, since God reveals his wonders to you in various ways. Then it behooves you to seek nothing except that your spirit be in this way affected and moved. Gaze at God by a single glance, preferring this to any pious and rousing considerations. Thus you will say your office in a divine manner, because we must more highly esteem God and our simple and agreeable affection by which we may purely and simply cling to Him than the profoundest and most abundant sentiments, laboriously acquired, whence come distractions and wanderings of the mind."

On the other hand meditation and contemplation greatly assist the recitation of the Divine Office and naturally lead up to it.

By the fact that Christ is the center of psalmody, as is evident from its connection with the eucharistic sacrifice, from the Messianic character of the Psalms, and from the liturgical cycle of feasts, we are more intimately united to Christ, and through love for Him we are excellently well fitted for contemplation,

After the consideration of all these points it is evident that the recitation of the Divine Office, particularly in choir, must be preferred to all private prayer. One Who understands and loves this "principal feature" of our Order and who realizes how important it is for his own spiritual life as well as for religion itself and for the proper celebration of the liturgy of the Church, will consider exemption from choir not a desirable privilege but a dire necessity and will discharge the Divine Office with his Brethren and will do his part to have the Office held in his Convent and to make its celebration possible. Unless our religious act so, a Carmelite community will hardly differ from a community of secular priests merely living in the same house and only assembling at a common table; and unless this is the case, a common meditation will likewise be omitted. There is no doubt that he who wishes and tries to be present at Divine Office usually suffers no loss in his other duties and apostolic works. More frequently it is not so much necessity as carefreeness and convenience that keep him from choir.

Examples are attractive:

"Father Michael of St. Augustine was always the first to hasten to Matins which among us are held at midnight, and in this he was so zealous that among the forty novices and young Professed who were together with us at Malines in 1668, not one was able ever to precede him, although many were very fervent and used to challenge one another to come most speedily to choir in order to steal from the rest the blessing of the Guardian Angel."

"Saint Mary Magdalen had a most ardent zeal in reciting the Divine Office. Therefore on the way to the choir she used to experience such joy of spirit that she seemed to be going to a splendid banquet. She was on the watch also that the divine praises be discharged devoutly and reverently; and if ever she found a sister going faster than was proper she was greatly annoyed, saying that she did not dare rush the divine praises as though they were exterior exercises of the monastery." She preferred presence in choir for recitation of Divine Office to any other devotion, prayer, and private meditation. If a Sister under such a pretext asked to be dispensed from choir she would say, "I believe I would be deceiving you, if I were to permit this, because if you think to honor and please God more in this private exercise, you will discover that you have not done it. For in comparison with the recitation of the Divine Office with the other Sisters, every other prayer is of little merit."

As long as the hours consecrated to prayer, whether mental or vocal, as the Divine Office, are faithfully observed in the monastery, there remains at least the skeleton of religious observance which can easily be brought back to life. But if the Superiors do not care even for these hours of prayer, nothing remains to save religious life and such a religious house is of necessity desecrated.

For these reasons it will at once be clear to an attentive observer that no good can come to an Order from small houses in which on account of the scarcity of religious nothing of what we have been writing can be observed.

Such houses create the danger that the religious who have dwelt a long time in them become accustomed to their liberty and when they are once more transferred to larger houses they allege a thousand and one reasons and refuse to go, or if they do go they are a source of scandal and a hindrance rather than of help and edification. If the number of small houses in a Province exceeds the number of large ones, nothing else is possible but the ruin of discipline in the entire Province; and no matter how zealous the Superior may be for regular discipline, he is held and compelled to put up with all evils, no matter how serious.

Not without reason do our Constitutions warn us: —"Our Communities shall proceed very cautiously in accepting pious foundations so that they may not be too easy in accepting burdensome ones and such as would demand some change in the usual order of regular discipline." How much more true is this in the foundation of a new house! It is by no means sufficient that the letter of the law be saved and that the necessary funds are on hand or at least confidently expected; before all things it must be proved that regular observance will remain intact both in the Province and in the new house. The Rule has good reason for demanding that the places should be suitable, "ad vestrae religionis observantiam apta."

What advantage is there in opening new houses when those already existing do not correspond to the Carmelite spirit? What advantage in creating new life, if the old life is to be killed? Indeed the Order cannot grow except like a tree, i.e., not by force, but according to the order of nature and with the help of divine grace.

We shall not, either, carry with us the blessing of God into our new houses, if regular life in the old houses or in the whole Province is on their account destroyed, since indeed all depends on such a blessing. That foundation cannot be either according to the will of God which must always and everywhere be sought, or for the glory of God and the salvation of souls. Perhaps a few years later the matter will be so evident that even those at present unconvinced will also believe.

SECTION THREE

The Exercise of the Presence of God

HUMAN nature and the demands of life do not permit us to remain continuously in meditation and contemplation. Our Rule insinuates as much when besides prayer it inculcates work to avoid idleness, "ad evitandan otiositatem." Nevertheless it is not lawful to drop prayer in order to work, since according to the Lord's teaching one must always pray and not grow faint. Even though prayer cannot always burst forth in a flame, yet the spark must always and everywhere be shielded so that on occasions it may be easily fanned into a real fire. Every effort should be made to have the habitual union with God become actual.

Our Rule teaches this very thing, since Chapter XVI in demonstrating the spiritual armor urges "that the sword of the Spirit which is the word of God should dwell abundantly in our hearts, and whatsover we have to do, let it be done in the word of the Lord." To the hours given to prayer and scattered among our other occupations, it is necessary to add the practice of the presence of God, that when we have given ourselves to the active life, the "pars principalior," our special feature, may be preserved and not lose its proper place.

"In this continual, active and affectionate discourse with God," to quote the Methodus Orandi, "chiefly is found the spirit of our holy Order according to those words of our holy Rule, 'Meditating day and night on the law of the Lord.' " For the word "meditating" does not mean that we must always be occupied in actually meditating and in examining divine things. This is impossible for the weakness of the human spirit and mind; but by it we must understand the affection of our heart and the fervor of our will which is not only not wearied by loving as the mind is by thinking; but rather, on the contrary, the more it loves, the more attraction, pleasure and strength does it feel to keep on loving more and more. In this respect, without doubt, the spirit of our holy Order is by far the most sublime, and our brethren should value it most highly, because it is the most excellent heritage that could accrue to anyone in this world. We are called to that state in which we profess to practice a life of prayer, and this life is the most perfect imitation of the life led by the Blessed in heaven.

And again: "There is no more efficacious means of keeping our mind recollected and ready to speak to God than always to walk in the presence of God. The practice of God's presence must be highly prized by those of our Order, because through it our holy father Elias worked such miracles in this world and he left this practice to his holy disciple Eliseus together with his double spirit as a most precious legacy. 'The Lord liveth in whose presence I stand.' " This practice of the divine presence if understood fully, i.e., if united to pious affections, keeps our minds and hearts riveted on God even amidst the manifold distractions of the active life and it guarantees that we shall return promptly and gladly to true and perfect prayer at the appointed times. By it our works are made holy and fruitful.

Our Constitutions exhort to this practice quite generally. They say that the novice-master should repeatedly instruct the novices not only about meditating and examining their conscience, but also about the various ways of praying and of directing their acts together with the practice of the presence of God so that afterwards they may be lovers of the interior life and, as far as God grants it, actually practice it according to the Rule.

A proper place and time should be given the professed clerics so that they may proceed to the interior life according to the dispositions of each.

Likewise the Father who has the charge, should teach the lay-brothers a method of prayer and of directing their acts together with the practice of the divine presence.

If this exercise is of the highest importance for the spiritual life of all, it is necessary in a special way for a Carmelite; and he who refuses to practice it as far as he can, does not fulfill the precept of our Rule about continuous meditation. In fact, the very periods of meditation without this exercise have little value in daily life, since they are ill applied, or they have no influence on daily life. By this exercise the fire lighted by meditation and contemplation is preserved until the next period of prayer. It is likewise the channel in which the water drawn in meditation and contemplation is led down to the individual occupations and periods to help in our own and others' salvation.

Father Michael of St. Augustine holds that mystical theology comprises only two parts, "namely, a living faith in the divine presence in every place and in every creature and a real conformity of our will with the divine." Moreover, he very thoroughly and profoundly explains and teaches this exercise.

S. Mary Magdalen de Pazzi deemed it highly necessary to see that her disciples had their hearts fixed on God. Frequently she asked them, "Where is your heart just now? In what is it occupied? Of what is it thinking? How often have you thanked God today for having called you to his Order? For having given Himself to you today in the Eucharist?" By these and similar devices she used to accustom them to keep their hearts occupied with God, to pay attention to His interior voice, to keep before their eyes the presence of God, to converse with Him, and always to walk with an open heart, saying that she herself from her tenderest years had experienced how great a help such practices were.

CHAPTER III

The Contemplative Life

Necessary Conditions

NO CARMELITE will condemn our teaching about mental prayer and the practice of the divine presence; neither will any Carmelite be found who would not wish to put it into practice. Greater difficulties, however, will arise from the consequences of our doctrine,—consequences required or supposed as conditions sine qua non for a life dedicated to prayer. How does it happen that so many religious make so little progress in meditation and contemplation? Why is the practice of the divine presence begun so fervently and then gradually dropped?

No one will say that this happens because mental prayer and the exercise of the divine presence are too difficult. Because even rude and uncultured men have learned them and have reached the highest degrees. Neither will anyone object that little if any fruit is reaped therefrom and that too great sacrifices are placed on us, since through them the yoke of God is usually made sweet and light and great joy and consolation usually spring from them.

In truth, the real reason is that in order that interior prayer may be permanent and flourish, it makes certain demands not infrequently displeasing to human nature. For there are required solitude, silence, mortification and self-denial. "Do you wish to know," says Father Michael of St. Augustine, "how the spirit of prayer is to be cultivated and preserved? I see three requirements before all others, namely, solitude, silence, and mortification."

SECTION ONE

On Solitude

WHO HAS not experienced how easy it is to pray and to speak with God in retirement? Has not our holy father Elias taught this? Have not our holy fathers taught it when for this very reason they betook themselves to Mt. Carmel? For the same reason our Rule prescribes that all should remain in their cells or at least near them (at that time one cell was removed some distance from its neighbor). Likewise the Rule seems to prefer "loca in eremis," places in solitudes, and commands that each religious should have a separate cell. This precept our Constitutions have preserved, not, mark it well, for the convenience of the individual religious, but that we may converse more easily with God according to the gift received from the Holy Ghost.

Since we are accustomed to call our monasteries other Carmels, we must not forget that Mount Carmel denotes solitude, as the Rule of John 44 explains. Every Carmelite monastery should exhibit this characteristic of solitude, even though the Order has ceased to be eremitical, unless we should wish to affirm that the Order has essentially changed and has preserved not even the slightest vestige of its primitive character and spirit. In this case we must confess that the name itself means nothing.

Without doubt the active life to which we have been transplanted makes it impossible for us to imitate our forefathers in their perfect retirement, and no one expects this from us. Still, all Carmelites who love to speak with God and who consider such speech as our chief portion, must be ardent in their love of solitude. If one finds his enjoyment in profane conversations and seeks them unnecessarily, he cannot earnestly desire conversation with God. To seek God only when we grow weary of men is highly unbecoming, especially for Carmelites. He who without necessity or true usefulness despises the Constitutions, neglects his duties and spurns the company of his brethren to frequent the homes of seculars, can hardly be judged acting out of pure zeal for souls. How many religious have deceived themselves, and did not see, yes, did not even wish to see, that they were yielding to the wiles of human nature!

In the Constitutions published by order of the General Chapter held in Cremona in 1593, we read: "Since nothing is more opposed to reform than that our religious should be walking about in the cities and towns, through the squares and public places, we command the Reverend Prior not to grant permission for going out more than once a week. If, however, necessity should arise, so that one or several need dispensation, the Prior having investigated the matter well, may be lenient with one or the other in this particular case. However, no permission for going out should be allowed on feast days except for a very evident and reasonable cause."

John Baptist Rossi had already ordered: "Those of our regulars not appointed for some public business or to administer the sacraments, may not go out of the monastery except once a week, except in case of necessity. Nevertheless the Rev. Prior or the Senior can dispense in the case of some of good name and virtue, so that they may go out of the monastery twice a week."

The Constitutions of the Reform of Tours in the year 1637 order: "Since we are especially bound to retirement by our Rule, it is strictly forbidden to the Priors ever to give permission to visit rare spectacles, fine houses, or attractive gardens; the only permission granted our religious is for necessity, for assisting one's neighbor, and for doing lawful business." And elsewhere: "On Sundays and Holydays, Superiors must not under any conditions allow anyone to go out except to hold sermons or to listen to them, to hear confessions, to visit the sick, and to perform similar acts of charity then necessary. Likewise in Advent, in Lent and on Fridays it is lawful to go out even less frequently. At other times it may be allowed at most twice a week to those who ask permission, led by the motive of a simple and honest visit and of politeness."

Fr. Michael of St. Augustine who never forgets that we are now called to the active life, very well gives the following explanation: "It is indeed true that as the best, choicest and the chief heritage of Carmelites is to converse with God, so their secondary and as it were accidental one, is to help their neighbor. On this account it frequently happens that obedience or charity engages us in exterior occupations either by withdrawing us for a time from the retirement of our cell and cloister, or by applying us to manual work inside the limits of our cloister.

"But nevertheless we must be solicitous to preserve interior solitude by not distracting ourselves too much and by every effort exciting and cultivating a fervent desire for solitude, even for exterior solitude. So it will happen that we shall bestir ourselves to accomplish our external occupations quickly, that we shall not protract the unnecessary, but rather extricate ourselves from useless affairs and always long for our cell. Here let those ask themselves how they satisfy their vocation and their obligations, those, I say, who can hardly pass an hour in their cell, who with their whole heart are eager for trips and walks, who without necessity, without utility, without obedience, look for, seek and cultivate, numerous acquaintances and familiarities with men, delight in visiting frequently and in being visited, to whom retirement is a prison and conversation with men delightful and agreeable. Surely such are only abortive Carmelites, since they do not satisfy their duty and do not live worthy of their vocation."

Accordingly our Constitutions forbid us to go out without asking and obtaining the Superior's permission; they allow no general permissions for going out except to the officials for the business pertaining to their office and they give warning as follows: "In visits of this kind our religious shall beware of using time lightly and uselessly in talks and conversations hardly religious and not conducive to edification. They shall not remain in these visits too long, and they shall not go to any other places than those permitted by the Prior." They threaten, too, "He who without necessity shall go to a place or by a route other than allowed by his permission, or he who exceeds the time granted him, shall be punished according to his fault."

It is the duty of the individual religious faithfully to observe all these points, but it is the special duty of the Superiors to see that they are observed. Let no one persuade himself that these points are slight, since they affect the very essence of our Order and its chief feature.

It is not sufficient to abstain as far as we can from association with seculars; it is necessary moreover that we guard solitude even inside our monastery. What advantage have we in avoiding the company of seculars, if we so much more freely seek the conversation of our brethren outside the time appointed? For, although the mitigation of Eugene IV as it is called is added to the famous seventh chapter of our Rule, viz., "At proper times the Brethren may freely and licitly stay or walk about in their churches, in their cloisters or in their surroundings," the spirit of our Rule does not on this account seem to be destroyed. For it said, "boris congruis," i.e., in those periods which are set aside for recreation, just as now it is ruled that such recreations take place about one hour after dinner and after supper. Our Rule has not been mitigated as far as continual prayer is concerned, and these recreations will not destroy the spirit of prayer if we obey the warnings of the Constitutions, "In the daily recreations all, both priests and clerics, must take part at the appointed places, and some conversations about pious, becoming and useful topics shall be held, and precautions taken against detractions."

Consequently let each one seek solitude in the monastery as far as his occupations will permit, and let him not withdraw others from their solitude or disturb them without necessity. For our Constitutions expressly make this prohibition: "It is not lawful for anyone of any rank whatsoever, even though he is a guest, to enter the cell of another, especially during strict silence, without the Superior's permission. An exception is made in the case of Superiors and of officials for business entrusted to them. So much the more should strangers never be admitted in the cells without the Superior's permission."

In truth one's cell is not a place for recreation but for prayer; it is not a profane, but a holy place

SECTION TWO

Silence

SILENCE must necessarily be added to solitude so that the human mind can be elevated to God and can fly to Him. "All agree," says Fr. Michael of St. Augustine, "that silence is certainly necessary for the interior and mystical life." All spiritual writers affirm this and it is not difficult to see that they are right. Wherefore the Rule as well as the Constitutions command a certain strict silence which we cannot break without sin. But even outside of this, "even though so strict an observance of silence is not kept, we command that no one may speak except at recreation time or for some just cause; because then the brethren may speak briefly, modestly and in a low voice."

Moreover in certain places silence must always be kept, i.e., in the choir, sacristy, refectory, cloister, corridor and cells. In these places silence is necessary in a special way either because of the place itself or on account of what is done there. At recreation time, according to the Rule of the mitigation granted by Eugene IV, the brethren may walk about in the cloister and talk together, yet "modestly," as the Constitutions add.

In the refectory, however, the Superior when a just cause occurs, can dispense, but he is again warned to do this according to these Constitutions, but rarely. For ordinarily the material action in the dining-room by which we take food and drink should be spiritualized in some way by those who are chiefly called to converse with God, since they nourish their souls also by fitting reading.

Most wisely our Constitutions warn that silence is broken not only by speech, but also by any noise which can disturb others. Thence Fr. Michael of St. Augustine concludes "that the brethren should be modest in gait, strangers to loud talking, and always intent not to cause noise in any way. Thus they will always in some measure be keeping silence."

We affirm that only by silence are our monasteries recognized as other Carmela, so that those houses in which silence is habitually neglected should be convinced that they have strayed entirely from the way and spirit of our fathers. When silence is condemned and neglected, Carmel is profaned, and sacriligiously usurps a name so holy. "All true Carme-lites," says Fr. Michael of St. Augustine, "should convince themselves that just as the first mark of the true Carmelite spirit is a love for solitude, so the second mark is anxiety for preserving silence. You will see that such anxiously flee and shrink from occasions of much talking. When they must speak, and silence cannot be kept according to substance, they are careful to keep it in their manner of speaking, not speaking louder than is proper."

When praising the obedience of Fr. Michael de la Fuente, his biographer writes: "Since the unanimous consent of our Carmelite religious and the very text of the Rule of the Carmelite Order show that the chief aim of the Order is to meditate day and night on the law of the Lord and since all ascetical writers unanimously teach that solitude and silence are the means toward this end not merely after a manner becoming but indispensably necessary, we can hardly describe how our Father Michael, consecrated as he was to prayer and the consideration of divine things, was anxious throughout his life about the observance of silence and solitude, virtues so recommended in the Rule. He was never seen anywhere except in his cell or in the choir. His confessor affirmed that he was not accustomed to speak, except a necessity of life, charity toward his neighbor, or obedience demanded it."

St. Mary Magdalen de Pazzi felt the same way. "Among our rules she esteemed holy silence most highly. She was accustomed to say that it was impossible for a religious soul to taste heavenly things, if she did not relish silence; but, she said, that such a one would always live in affliction and tribulation because many faults are committed by those who do not restrain their tongue."

Fr. Philip Thibault "also used to impress upon his novices that solitude and silence were the two characteristics by which a strong and flourishing Order could be distinguished from a weak and languishing one. In truth when he was Superior, so intense was the cultivation of these two virtues among all that his illustrious Lordship, Francis de L'Achivier, at that time Bishop of Rennes, was frequently lost in astonishment. When he came into the monastery and did not hear the religious chanting the praises of God in choir, he would ask where they were. When he heard that they were in their cells or at manual labor, 'Indeed,' he exclaimed, 'this surely is astonishing. Sixty to eighty religious live in this house, and so great is their retirement at midday, that it could be no greater at midnight.' This observance of silence so impressed him that he urged his only nephew whom he might have promoted to the highest ecclesiastical dignities, to forsake the world and to embrace our institute."

The requirements of the Rule and Constitutions cannot be satisfied by keeping only exterior silence unless one adds interior silence. "Exterior silence," we read in Fr. Michael of St. Augustine, "is, so to say, the remote preparation to acquire the Carmelite's most precious heritage. Furthermore, internal silence is the proximate disposition and the preparation most conducive to the interior life. Internal silence consists in the faithful soul's actually quieting and restraining the confusion and excessive activity of his whole interior and of his interior faculties. Man having imposed silence upon his imaginative and appetitive faculties and upon his other senses, by means of a careful suspension of their operations, holds himself intimately recollected in the inner part of his soul in order that he may be able to perceive in it the voice of God talking to his heart. A true Carmelite, therefore, strives to procure for himself such silence in order that by doing all things in such silence he may proximately dispose himself for mystic union with his heavenly Spouse and for continual interior conversation with Him."

After these explanations, it is quite clear how greatly an occupation in one's cell which nourishes the worldly spirit rather than the religious, is removed from our chief aim; and how keeping in one's cell such objects as in these our days usually please seculars, is removed from the perfection of Carmel. What do you think when any and every matter is allowed to enter a monk's cell by means of radio, even though the doors are closed, and strict silence has begun? Is it not right and proper that so many Orders and Congregations whose chief aim is not continual prayer, have completely forbidden the private use of the radio?

Yes, he does not seem to observe religious silence, who, not compelled by any necessity and not impelled by any higher motive than his pleasure, wastes his time in profane reading, because our Rule orders us to remain in our cells, not that we may enjoy ourselves privately, but that we may entertain ourselves with God. Even though the term occupation must now be understood in a wider sense, so that any study of S. Theology, of Philosophy and the other sciences, fulfills the precept of the Rule, especially if undertaken for the better understanding of Theology or Holy Scripture or for promoting the glory of God and the good of our neighbor, still we must be careful that our minds be not completely carried away from God and things divine by these occupations.

Yet there are certain occupations which even a good intention cannot hinder from inflaming our heart with an immoderate love for creatures and from shutting up our ears to the divine call.

Blessed John Soreth very well explains what silence imports. "May there be silent among us," he says, "the abusive tongue, the blaspheming tongue the exaggerating tongue. How good it is to wait for God's salvation in such silence! Yet be silent in such a way, that you be not completely silent; be not silent with God. Speak to him in praise against boasting to obtain pardon for the past. Speak to Him in thanksgiving against murmuring to find forgiveness in the future. Speak to Him earnestly in petition so that He may never cease forgiving, granting, and promising."

One reason perhaps why so many religious become weary of solitude and silence is that they have never discovered, and have never tried to discover, what silence and solitude are for. Thus they have never experienced how sweet the Lord is, nor how all delights are surpassed by the sweetness of prayer. Another reason is that they confound a life of solitude with laziness and consider it useless for the world. We may disregard the fact that true prayer is not sloth or idleness, but rather is very necessary in our days for the life and salvation of the world; yet many projects can be launched in the solitude of one's cell, many deeds accomplished of which the world at large and our Order stand in need. Here likewise charity must begin with ourselves.

If our forefathers had not been greater lovers of silence and solitude than we, we should not now possess those books from which the tradition and glory of Carmel are so evident. Indeed we, so addicted to external occupations and so taken up with the delight of modern books, seem hardly to recognize their books, so that frequently we draw unnecessarily from others, ignoring and despising our own sources. Frequently, alas, Carmelite life is the loser!

Ordinarily we are not so pleased with work to be done for the Order within the walls of the monastery and nature itself urges us to external works, because we expect to be buoyed up occasionally by the applause and friendship of men.

"Let us therefore keep silence," warns Bl. Soreth, "because continuous silence and a lasting separation from the voice of seculars, compel us to meditate on heavenly things."

Whoever has learned to hear the voice of God in silence and solitude, will also obey as soon as he is called away by God to labor among men, whereas others who do not hear the voice of God or who neglect it, usually follow their natural inclinations and their passions. A man zealous for solitude on account of God, promptly forsakes God on account of God, in order that he may serve God in men.

SECTION THREE

On Mortification

CONCERNING mortification Fr. Michael of St. Augustine writes as follows: "Nobody can deny that the unceasing practice of mortification in all things is absolutely necessary for the interior life. To lead an interior life great purity of heart is required since it is written, 'Blessed are the clean of heart for they shall see God.' The interior life, such as is particularly becoming to a Carmelite, consists chiefly in a loving vision or contemplation of God, present always and everywhere, and working all things in all."

Many, it is true, long after the interior life and begin the practice of God's presence very fervently and yet do not persevere because they will not deny themselves, even though they experience the necessity of denying themselves. Accordingly they take refuge in a more active life, hoping that their desires will be more easily fulfilled. Unless one renounces all that he possesses and denies himself he cannot be a disciple of the Lord and cannot taste what the

Lord has prepared for those who love Him, because he has a heart not pure enough and a taste not upright enough.

Wherefore, says the Rule of John 44, "in order that we may attain the gifts of perfection and of promised glory, we must be careful to study the pattern given by God to the blessed Elias. For God speaking to Elias tells each hermit monk both of the Old and the New Law, "Recede hinc," Depart hence, namely, from uncertain and fleeting things of the world; "et vade contra orientem," and go to the east, i.e., against the natural desires of your flesh; "et abscondere in torrente Carith," and hide in the torrent Carith, i.e., do not dwell with the crowds in cities. "Qui est contra Jordanem," which is over against the Jordan, i.e., that thou mayest be separated from your faults by means of charity. Rising by these four steps to the height of prophetic perfection, "ibi de torrente bibis," thou shalt drink of the torrent.

From this teaching the Rule of St. Albert does not differ. It is constantly urging Carmelites to perfect renunciation, abnegation and mortification. It places obedience as the principle of all Carmelite life, and in the very first chapter demands that it be promised to the Prior and then executed in reality and truth. A Carmelite, therefore, must before all things renounce his own will; because the contemplative life, as history shows, is open to continual and most harmful illusions, unless it is directed by lawful authority. Moreover, no sacrifice will be pleasing to God, if we keep our own will; and God will not communicate Himself to a soul, which by its very conduct refuses to acknowledge that obedience is better than sacrifices.

For this reason, St. Mary Magdalen would do nothing either publicly or privately to win her Superiors' way of thinking to her own; but she conformed her will with theirs. And when someone would say to her that she would be frequently kept from prayer and interior converse with God on account of community exercises she said that it was her belief that even the slightest community exercise would be more pleasing to God than the most sublime contemplation. Thus it was that when she was rapt in ecstasy and the Mother Prioress would say to her, "Sister Mary Magdalen, come at once to this or that exercise," she would at once return to her senses, and promptly execute the order of obedience.

To obedience, is added poverty, since "none of the Brothers should claim anything as his own; but all things should be common to Carmelites and should be distributed to each by the Prior."

He who seeks this one thing necessary need not worry about accidentals, because then he seeks first the kingdom of God and His justice. We cannot cling to both creatures and the Creator, neither can we lean to both sides. Consequently poverty is to be esteemed most highly and observed most exactly in the Order of Carmel. And it is by no means enough to have merely a knowledge of what one is obliged to do under sin. It is not lawful to think that we have accomplished everything, if we have gotten the permission of our Superior in some way, even though it is a question of superfluities. But on account of contemplation we must aspire to the virtue of poverty which consists in an entire freedom from all creatures, so that we do not even cherish an inordinate desire of creatures.

Fr. Michael of St. Augustine penned the following beautiful words: "To give a short description: Carmelite or perfect poverty is nothing else than a voluntary renunciation of everything which is not God, excluding every human affection for any creature which one might call his own or which is not possessed in God or according to Him. Moreover, this renunciation requires that man possess nothing even by desire, that he yearn for nothing, that he rest in nothing, that he strip himself of every creature. It requires that one remain in some way in God, without will, knowledge, understanding or feeling for any created thing, even for divine gifts (charisms) insofar as one might be able to intend or to admit in them something as his own or his own satisfaction outside of God.

"The reason, however, why so entire a renunciation of all things is required is that every creature, no matter how excellent, may hinder the immediate union of the soul to God, if possessed with attachment or ownership. As long as the soul is not stripped of all things, it cannot be essentially or immediately united with God. All true Carmelites must strive after this poverty of spirit; for since it is their vocation to converse constantly and lovingly with God and to be in a special way united with Him by the bond of perfect charity, they are also obliged to use the proper means for this, among which poverty of spirit, which we have just described, is the chief. Yes, I am convinced that a true Carmelite must strive for such a degree of perfection that he will gradually learn to live among creatures as though they did not exist." How correctly he writes! since St. Gregory teaches that all things are small to him who sees their Creator.

For the same reason St. John planned to lead souls to "nada," nothingness, where, after creatures had been rejected, God might be all in all. The Venerable John of St. Samson preached nothing less than that we should entirely die to ourselves. So thought our Saints who begged as their reward "to suffer and to be despised," or who even preferred to die.

Such a spirit is not different from simple and perfect trust in God the preacher of which St.

Therese of the Child Jesus proclaimed herself to be. All these examples tend to prove one thing, i.e., that having renounced all creatures and even ourselves we must cling entirely to God, desiring and awaiting only His good will.

Consequently our Constitutions very properly call holy poverty the foundation of religious perfection and exhort and beseech in the Lord, "that all love it, preserve it in its purity, and experience it in its effects, after the example of our Redeemer, who when he was rich was made poor."

Moreover, they teach, "None of the Brethren should dare keep as their own anything that has been granted them for use, or to accept or give or exchange anything of value without the permission of the Superior." Indeed, every year on the occasion of renewal of vows the Superior must by formal precept make sure "that every one turn over to the Community whatever goods of value he may have without due permission."

In this way every appearance of ownership or of a private purse is excluded and there seems to be no necessity to add these words of the Tours Constitutions: "In order that the occasion and even the excuse for ownership may be radically excluded from our Order we strictly forbid the establishment of any common strong-box in which monies are to be kept or even anything else with the mark or name of some religious for his special use. Although such use can be licit by common law, practically it is very harmful; and if anyone should introduce this custom or shall tolerate it, he is to be deposed from office; he must be considered disqualified for office and moreover he is to be most severely punished."

Besides our Constitutions prescribe, as they ought, perfect community life, and close the chapter on poverty with this warning, "Finally, we strictly forbid that anyone should be elected to any office, if he does not observe perfect community life with regard to poverty; otherwise the election by law itself is null and void."

Then lest poverty should become useless by a merely technical and juridical interpretation and by easily granted permissions, the Constitutions say, "On this condition shall permission be given that those things allowed the Brethren for their use, be not too choice, but simple and of moderate price." And, "In the cells of the Brethren the furniture should be simple, uniform and entirely in keeping with religious poverty; therefore we forbid our religious to keep in their cells superfluities, especially such as show a worldly rather than a religious spirit."

Bl. John Soreth has affirmed, "No regular prelate should think that he can dispense one of his subjects in the matter of ownership; because the renouncing of ownership, just like the keeping of chastity, is so joined to the Rule of an Order, that not even the highest authority can dispense in it." In fact in order that no one may cling inordinately to his cell, the Superior may change the cells of the Brethren as he pleases.

Bl. John Soreth makes the following annotation to Chapter III of our Rule which treats of the cells: "He does not say palaces which are huge buildings in which they can move about, but cells, 'cellulas,' the diminutive of 'cella,' as though he would say 'Let each one have a little cell.'"

Those, therefore, err who imagine that the vow of poverty is satisfied when the technicality of permission is observed, and yearn after all the conveniences of our age just like seculars, as regards our buildings, cells and furnishings. They likewise err, who think that all things are lawful while traveling, forgetful of these words of our Constitution:

"Although Superiors out of fraternal charity must anticipate the wants of the Brethren who are traveling and must diligently supply those things that are necessary for the trip, still subjects should beware of spending money received from Superiors or others for purposes and purchases of superfluous and useless objects." For according to what we have seen, Carmelite religious desire and work, not that they may have all that others have; but that they may have few needs and having freed themselves completely from creatures and so found peace, they may freely and more tranquilly give themselves to God and cling to Him. Our chief prerogative so demands.

Our forefathers understood this very well and put it into practice. In the life of Father Michael de la Fuente we read: "The second sapling which sprang from the root of humility was a love of poverty and accompanying it a perpetual refusal of all personal comforts and a universal contempt of earthly things. If you will except a few cheap cardboard pictures and a few books for study, he had no furnishings in his room but some terrible scourges, hair shirts, and a mattress stuffed with stones instead of felt. He never had money, unless by chance he would occasionally accept some alms from the faithful to give to the unknown poor or surely to the poorest of the poor. If at times the rich paid something for the Scapulars he gave them, in place of giving an alms, he would act as though it were a sin to touch money, and asked that it be given to the layman who accompanied him in his apostolic journeys, that it might keep him and his companion while on the way."

St. Mary Magdalen de Pazzi wishing to instruct her sisters in the imitation of the Bl. Virgin Mary was accustomed to say, "We should be rightly called the sisters of the Bl. Virgin, if weary in the evening from our labors, we should find someone to ill treat us and to welcome us with blows instead of food and rest. O how fortunate we should be, if we should sit down to table and not find anything to eat; if we should look for sleep, and not find a place to put our head!" Fr. Michael of St. Augustine who tells these things himself, continues: "Behold, dearly beloved, the best way to be called the Brothers of the Blessed Virgin; namely, after her example freely to suffer want and the inconveniences of poverty. In truth, we ought the more rejoice, the more our food tastes of poverty; and the more our clothes show strenuous use, the more pleasing they should be to us. In this strain St. Mary Magdalen de Pazzi so well said that the cheaper and poorer the goods of the monastery are, the more precious they must be considered and the more in conformity with holy poverty."

St. Brocard exhorted his brethren from his death-bed, "Therefore, remain constant in good. Execrate riches, despise the world, and model an upright life after the pattern of Mary and Elias."

It will be of great advantage to us to meditate well on those things which we read in the life of Fr. Philip Thibault, the true founder of the Reform of Tours. "He did not willingly accept foundations with perpetual or annual incomes. First, because he especially wished to establish the Reform in a more perfect poverty so that it might depend entirely on Divine Providence and so that he might be able to say with greater truth and confidence, 'Give us this day our daily bread.' Second, because he feared, as frequently happened, that foundations with obligations might prove harmful to regular life which ought to be uniform and unvarying in the various houses of the same reform. One schedule fits regular life; another fits the lay people to whom we are obligated by the foundations made by them. Finally yielding to the wishes of the community he accepted some larger foundations in order that the extreme want of his houses might be alleviated, as I heard him say. Yet it happened to us, as I have seen it happen to other Orders; when we had nothing, Providence supplied our necessities abundantly; now, however, when we do have some property, Providence has become rare and frequently necessities are lacking."

Wherefore not only individual religious but the entire community must always respect poverty, and it is not lawful to believe that we shall reap greater fruits in the Lord's vineyard by a greater assimilation to the spirit of the world and to the customs of the age. The Lord Himself called the Apostles to extreme poverty, since they would be the more prompt to go whenever and wherever they might be sent by the Lord, the freer and more detached they would be from created things.

The true Carmelite life also embraces personal mortification, because no one can observe obedience and poverty according to the letter and spirit of the vows unless he is truly mortified and dead to himself. Sins against the vows reveal a lack of mortification rather than ignorance about them. For the rest, the soul can hardly meditate and contemplate the things of God in all tranquillity if it is continually being disturbed and excited by the passions. Consequently, St. Thomas and the other theologians affirm that the moral virtues are necessary dispositions for the contemplative life.

Our Rule, just like the rules of other contemplative Orders, prescribes quite severe corporal mortifications. If we omit the austerity which made our forefathers live in caves and not in cells as we do, the primitive Rule, prescribes protracted and very severe fasts and abstinences, and on exempt days they hardly imitated Dives, but rather poor Lazarus.

Neither is anyone ignorant how highly fasting has always been esteemed by spiritual authors and by those striving after perfection. We shall quote the words of Bl. John Soreth from his Exposition of the Carmelite Rule, "Fasting is good and salutary, because everlasting punishments are wiped out when sin is forgiven. It is not only a removal of sin, but also the eradication of vice. Not only does it obtain forgiveness, but also merits grace. Not only does it blot out sins of the past, but it guards against future sins which we might commit."

He gives a most beautiful explanation how prayer and fasting mutually assist each other. "I have only one thing yet to say, fasting adds devotion and confidence to prayer. Behold how prayer and fasting accompany each other! Prayer obtains the strength to fast; and fasting the grace to pray. Fasting strengthens prayer, and prayer sanctifies the fast and presents it to God. Of what good is fasting if confined to earth? Be this far from us, and let fasting be raised to God on the wings, as it were, of prayer. But lest not even this should suffice, it is necessary to add even another help. Let us therefore have two wings for our fasting that it may penetrate heaven, i.e., assiduous prayer and justice which grants everyone his due."

Since the time of Eugene IV this severity of our Rule has been much softened; but even after the mitigation there have always flourished in our Order those who were addicted to fasting.

Fr. Michael de la Fuente was accustomed on Fridays to eat only bread and some legumes mixed with gentian and aloe, and never to quench his thirst except perhaps to moisten his lips. For three hours he would chew a piece of gentian raw; and how bitter this is, two novices had occasion to learn! One out of a spirit of mortification tasted it pure; another out of curiosity tasted it mixed with other herbs. Both confessed that for three days they were unable to rid their palate of the bitterness and disagreeableness of that taste.

Ven. Angelus Paoli was a shining example of temperance on account of his abstinence from food and drink. In the morning he usually ate some herbs and some legumes, bitter and badly seasoned. With the Superior's permission he abstained from the portion usually given at table to each religious, and gave it to the poor; or he would exchange it for two loaves of bread and give these to the poor. In the evening, however, he was never seen to bring food or drink to his lips. He hardly ever accepted an invitation to dinner; but when he did, he went gladly, but ate most sparingly. With his mind always intent on his poor he would ask for a part of those foods that could be kept, for the relief of the poor. Finally, so great was his abstinence, though he tried to conceal it, that he was only skin and bones. It was considered marvelous that a man so emaciated by fastings, could bear so many labors and inconveniences. Sometimes to please his friends or to conceal his abstinence he would eat a little more than usual; but the next day he would atone for this slight indulgence shown his body by means of rigorous fasts and mortifications.

The Constitutions, as we may expect, follow the mitigated Rule. But lest we be unnatural children of our forefathers, we must so much more faithfully observe and guard whatever remains of their austerity and courage.

Although there may be reasons why one or the other should be dispensed from fasting, it is not lawful to minimize and disregard the law of fasting on principle, or to think that each and every one of our day is ipso facto excused. In fact, a dispensation may not be sought on this plea.

One burning with zeal for souls will often strive to strengthen his apostolic labors by means of fasting. For many kinds of demons are not cast out except in prayer and fasting.

If someone by chance really cannot keep the fast, he ought to try to supply in some other way, in order that he may not be deprived of the reward of fasting or be found a stranger to the spirit of Carmel. The best fast would be to do without those things which are of little or no value to health, or which not infrequently are harmful to health. Since the indulgence in such practices does not seem to accord with religious poverty and the spirit of renunciation, they have come to be forbidden in many religious Orders. Here is our chance, here is our duty!

The other regulations which our Constitutions propose are likewise very useful to promote the spirit of mortification, viz., "Our brethren including Superiors shall eat of like food at a common table, unless illness known to the Superior should excuse." "Food and drink shall not be served to anybody outside of regular meals, except with permisison of the Superiors."

The Rule has been changed, as is known, by these words of Innocent IV: "You shall eat together in a common refectory those things that have been distributed to you." Lezana explains this chapter thus: "It is inferred from these words that four precepts are given us. First, that we should not eat outside the refectory; second, that the meal should be taken together; third, that no special food should be served in this place; fourth, that at mealtime some reading from Sacred Scripture should take place, where this point can be carried out." In this way both poverty and mortification are observed; and he who is resolved never to eat outside the refectory either with seculars or in his cell, follows the Rule perfectly.

The Rule does not explicitly mention other kinds of mortification, as hair shirts, disciplines, a hard bed, etc. But our forefathers were accustomed to use garments that were as rough and poor as hair shirts and they do not seem to have known soft beds. Many matters of this kind needed no special mention or recommendation among the hermits of those days and regions, because they were taken for granted in the religious, and especially, in the eremitical life. Besides, our Rule admonishes us not to forget works of supererogation, which according to the teaching of the Ven. John of St. Samson are meant to refer to our external life and not to our internal, which being consecrated entirely to God, admits of no works of supererogation.

In the history of the Order we find many wonderful examples of such supererogatory works and of voluntary mortification. We may omit what our well-known saints and such men as Fr. Michael de la Fuente and the Ven. Angelus Paoli practiced, giving only the example of Fr. Philip Thibault who added mortification to prayer, realizing that although these were distinct virtues, one could not exist without the other. For four years during which he was engaged in higher studies, he took no other rest than stretched upon the hard floor. To such a hard couch he added an inhuman scourging three times a week. He frequently wore a hair shirt or a belt woven with sharp points, and he wished it established by law that in all our houses there should be on hand instruments of this kind for mortifying the body.

In fact, we read in the Constitutions of the Reform of Tours published in 1642, "Although a large part of our profession consists in chastising the flesh which is prescribed everywhere in our house regulations and in these Constitutions, nevertheless we urge upon our brethren to embrace whatever may be disagreeable to the body, both in food and in clothing, in order that they may more and more conquer the movements of sensuality and so fix their souls on God. For this purpose there should be found in each convent hair shirts, shirts and belts interwoven with knots and bristles, iron chains suitable for girding the waist, and similar instruments suitable for mortifying the body. They are to be kept in the Prior's and the novice-master 's cell, so that anyone may use them, but only with their permission. Each one should have his own discipline made of cords."

Fr. Thibault, continues Fr. Licinius, carefully observed the fasts of the Church and of the Order. Although he preached every day in Advent and in Lent, he would under no condition lesson his austerities or his customary prayers. Behold an apostolic man, and likewise after the example of our holy fathers, a man of prayer, an ardent lover of mortification,—in a word a true Carmelite!

Article 108 of our present Constitution preserves the teachings of those Constitutions. Likewise all that is contained in chapter XVI, "The manner of life within our Convents," is directed toward this one end, and not only tends to the practice of decorum, but if faithfully observed, also to mortification and to the free and tranquil recollection of our mind in God.

Even assiduity in work which our Rule commands so strongly to all, can and must be considered mortification, especially since the Rule enjoins work, not so much to make a living,—those men needed little enough—but to avoid idleness and to overcome temptations. That religious, therefore, acts wrongly, who weary of mortification, shuns labors, or undertakes only such as are less tiring and molestful.

Finally our fathers were not ignorant of the fact that corporal mortification is of no value unless aided by interior mortification or self-denial. Indeed external mortification is the chief means to internal mortification, not to mention its expiatory and meritorious qualities and its power to implore graces and benefits from God. Whosoever will subdue his body, will the more easily subdue his interior passions and carry the yoke of the Lord.

Our Rule inculcates this interior and perfect abnegation and mortification in Chapter XVI where it teaches the use of spiritual arms in order that we may stand against the snares of the enemy and do all things in God's name. No one has followed this teaching more faithfully than the blind John of St. Samson who warns us that we must die entirely to ourselves so that we may live for God and in God.

This master was well understood by his disciple, Fr. Dominic of St. Albert, (1634) Vicar-Provincial of the Province of Tours who abundantly enjoyed graces really mystical in nature. "He was so given to mortification," writes Timothy of the Presentation, "that he always had this word upon his tongue and executed it in practice, 'I die daily.' Indeed he favored himself in nothing, so that if he should be inclined to sneeze he checked himself, striving even in this way to avoid negligence. When asked in a letter by the Ven. Br. John of St. Samson what he would consider the best thing in life he answered that he preferred to be humbly crucified with Holy Job on a dunghill, and to suffer persecution from heaven, the demons and men, rather than to convert nations to God with St. Paul in all his glory.

"He very sincerely confessed to his master, 'Do you know that we have become so accustomed to die that we prefer to suffer than to act?' He likewise confessed that sometimes he had been left by the Lord in such sadness and anxiety that this was noticeable to his brethren. But he likewise promises to try to show himself so much the more cheerful in future as he feels inwardly desolate. And in fact his biographer says: 'He always had a countenance modestly cheerful and smiling and never overcast by a cloud of sadness.' He bore terrible sufferings, when out of obedience and by duty he was called to teach theology, although drawn most vehemently by mystic graces to God and to continuous contemplation. 'Nevertheless,' he says, 'I am delighted with this death which I always consider better than life or corporal death. If I live in God, I desire death and I shall never find a better death than this one in which there is no relief, but in which we are neither dead nor alive, since we really seem not to exist at all.' "

And again, "Do you know what good corporal sufferings are to me? It seems to me, that I may be lifted up over all things. Bodily death is nothing, but the soul by reason of continuous severe pains is compelled to be always on the alert to keep itself in calmness with a serene countenance. We conquer our sufferings, when we bear them with joy, and when inwardly we seem to be in hell but outwardly we show ourselves most joyful. Thus our very pains which to others seem slight, increase our merit. This one thing I ask of God, that he may consume me with sufferings." We need not wonder how such men reached the highest mystical union. This is the glory of Carmel and its choicest calling.

CHAPTER IV

The Active Life in Carmel

WE READ in Fr. Michael of St. Augustine: "So far we have shown how Carmelites are bound to strive after purity of heart and a continual conversation with God in order that according to the teaching of John 44 Patriarch of Jerusalem they may in some little way anticipate in their heart and perceive in spirit the presence of God and the sweetness of heavenly glory,—and this not only after death, but even in this mortal life. But even though this is the chief aim of our prophetic institute, there is still another not so important, viz., to practice also the active life with the contemplative. This is so necessary that if anyone in our Order intended to practice only the active life, such as converting and instructing souls, in doing works of charity for our neighbor, in external occupations, he would not be a true Carmelite, inasmuch as he would lack the principal aim of our Order, namely, to converse interiorly with God in purity of heart; likewise if anyone would profess to follow only the contemplative life and would refuse to practice the active, such a one would not be a perfect Carmelite, but rather a hermit or a cenobite, because he lacks the active life, which is a partial, even though a less important phase of our institute. Although we have with Mary chosen the best part, viz., to sit at the feet of Jesus, which will not be taken from us, nevertheless we have also chosen the good part of Martha, that like her we may occasionally deign to be occupied with outside work when charity demands, or necessity compels, or obedience permits.

Our author derives this obligation of the active life from the words added by Innocent IV to the

Rule of St. Albert, "On Sundays or on other days when it shall be necessary you should treat of the observance of the rule, and the salvation of souls." These words he explains thus: "Surely by preaching, by hearing confessions, by winning sinners to penance, by visiting the sick, and by exercising other works of charity on our neighbors, as it is found necessary, and obedience allows, is meant to treat of the salvation of souls. Wherefore these works have been deservedly added by that Pontiff after we had been brought from the desert to work in the vineyard of the Lord."

This interpretation does not seem to correspond to the words, since in this place there is undoubtedly question of the chapter of faults, and of the salvation of the religious. So Bl. Soreth, Lezana and others affirm, and the Ven. John of St. Samson seemed to think that by these words the active life should be restricted as much as possible. There is no doubt, indeed, that our forefathers on Mt. Carmel applied themselves always and almost solely to contemplation. Still even at that time the apostolic life was not completely lacking, since so many apostolic labors are recorded in the lives of St. Cyril, St. Angelus, and others, and the imitation of the prophets Elias and Eliseus necessarily leads to the apostolic life. "If you desire," says Fr. Michael of St. Augustine, "a further proof of what we have said concerning this secondary aim of our Order, look at the life of our holy fathers Elias and Eliseus, and you will find that they joined the active with the contemplative life as is clearly evident from Holy Scripture in which the Holy Spirit has dictated the lives of these Saints."

All this becomes clearer after the Carmelites had migrated to Europe and were received among the mendicant Orders. Custom, the best interpreter of the law, has abundantly confirmed it, too. Thus, for many centuries the Constitutions explicitly, and quite generally mention the active life or suppose it.

Our Constitutions also establish the active life in article 2 in which they treat of the nature of our Order. In art. 827 they prescribe that the novice-masters should frequently teach that the spirit of our Order is a double one, i.e., not only the contemplative, but also the active. In article 60 they say that the active life "together with zeal for the salvation of souls undoubtedly constitute a true Carmelite."

No one will find any difficulty in admitting all that has been said. But in practice the active and the contemplative life are not so easily joined in such a way that neither shall suffer any loss, and that the contemplative life shall remain the chief feature from which the other will freely flow forth as from an abundant spring. "One thing is necessary," says Fr. Michael of St. Augustine, "to seek and to find a way to lead this double life without prejudice to either, ever mindful that to converse with God is the Carmelite's best heritage."

Carmelite perfection consists in the proper union and relationship between the active and the contemplative life. To reach it the following principles will have to be observed:

First. Always and everywhere the life of prayer and contemplation must in reality be esteemed and cultivated, by the entire Order, by the Superiors, by individual religious, as the foundation and most important feature of Carmelite life. In prayer the chief glory of our Order must always be seen and sought for. De facto, our Order is known in the Church, not so much for apostolic and external works, or for the sciences, in which without doubt we are excelled by other religious Orders, as for mystical theology in which St. Theresa and St. John of the Cross, the Mystical Doctor, were leaders.

"Mystical Theology," say our Constitutions, "is unquestionably the most excellent heritage of us Carmelites."

Thus not only men endowed with great talent and strength, should be esteemed and looked for, but also and in a special way, men truly contemplative, who do not refuse labor imposed by necessity or obedience; but who are drawn in an eminent way to God and interior things, and who really attain what the Rule of John 44 proposes as the aim of Carmelites. If, therefore, such a disposition is found in anyone, he should not be drawn more than necessary to exterior things, as both St. John of the Cross and the Ven. John of St. Samson, advise.

Oh, that the Order may not forget art. 112 in which eremitical Convents are recommended! Oh, that it be not merely to decorate the Constitutions!

If the Order honors only learned and very active men and tries to reward them with privileges and exemptions, and at the same time has less esteem for, and neglects men who are truly contemplative,—and here let me ask you not to mix these up with those who are lazy and tired of work,—it must frequently happen that spirits are quenched and completely destroyed to the loss of the Order and to the dishonor of God Himself whose sublime graces are deprived of their effect.

Therefore, each and every exercise prescribed by the Constitutions should be faithfully held in the Convents themselves; no religious should be dispensed or allowed to be absent for only trivial reasons. In spite of the many and great exterior occupations which at first sight seem to contradict one another, many points can be observed when a good spirit and the custom prevail in the Convent and are diligently fostered by the Superiors. Many points depend merely upon a proper schedule and the good will of the individual, since in those houses in which the spiritual exercises are usually neglected, frequently zeal for souls is also neglected. How can zeal for souls be born of contemplation and nurtured by it, as all writers demand, if contemplation itself is completely neglected and despised?

The Very Rev. Gabriel Wessels has written: "The truth that our spirit is a double one, should be impressed into the mind and heart from the beginning of the novitiate, so that it will stick for life. Otherwise it may happen that modern congregations which sometimes devote more time to spiritual exercises than many Mendicants do, perform better work in the Lord's vineyard, because their members were imbued with that spirit from the very beginning." In fact do not these recent Congregations accomplish better work just because they spend so much time in spiritual exercises, whence they are inflamed by true zeal, draw down the abundant blessing of God, and are not so much drawn away by their external work from union or conversation with God! For not every one who has joined a contemplative Order is a contemplative.

We heartily agree with our confrere when he says "It certainly is unworthy of a religious to be occupied in spiritual exercises for only two or three hours a day, and then for the rest of the day to do nothing." This is not the contemplative life, but sheer laziness which the Carmelite Rule so much abominates. Furthermore, we do not hesitate to affirm, that such religious do not properly apply themselves even to those few spiritual exercises; for if they did, they would surely realize that they must give themselves to God longer, in fact the whole day, or that they must be occupied usefully to satisfy the Rule, and not to misuse time granted them by God. Our Rule says with St. Paul, "if a man will not work, let him not eat." Fr. Wessels also correctly says that they who give themselves the whole day to the contemplative life, do a sublime work.

There is no danger that anyone will be hindered by contemplation itself from doing his duty, since obedience, charity and self-denial, are the foundation of contemplation, so that he who refuses to obey because of protracted contemplation should be under suspicion and should be recalled from contemplation by obedience.

The seraphic and ecstatic St. Mary Magdalen de Pazzi preferred rather to help her fellow-sisters who needed help than to spend her time in prayer and spiritual delights. Thus when once she was about to make the exercises of St. Ignatius, she omitted them. Asked the reason, she said, "I put God aside for His own sake." She had done this to assist a certain sister to whom an accident had happened. The services she performed for the lay-sisters in their work and in their company are beyond number. She exhausted her body doing as much by herself as was ordinarily done by four or more sisters. Steadily for six years she helped a lay-sister knead the bread. She herself would be the first to get up and begin the work, and like one of the lay-sisters she would carry in the bread on trays to put into the oven, although she had a very delicate constitution. She was nearly always with the lay-sisters not only to prepare the bread, but also in the laundry and for other services. When clothes had to be washed, she brought the kindling wood, and filled the kettles. Rising before the rest of the Convent, she lighted the fire, heated the lye, and began to wash. When she had others to help her, she always insisted on doing everything herself, in order to help the others.

Besides, all must be convinced that the apostolic labors of no one can be pleasing to God, if he should neglect his own salvation. He who has not remained in the vine, cannot give fruit, and God will not give increase, if man has not planted. For this reason all truly apostolic men cultivated prayer and union with God as much as they could, and the greater the tasks they were to undertake, the more they strove to converse with God, well aware of the fact that with God's assistance they would accomplish in a short time what otherwise would require a long time. Time is not wasted in prayer and meditation.

Indeed, Fr. Philip Thibault in the year 1615 before he committed to writing the practices of the Reform and drew them up in the form of Constitutions ordered silence and a retreat of ten days. He ordered the Blessed Sacrament to be exposed in the domestic chapel, before which each one had to spend an hour praying for the success of so important an undertaking in order to obtain light from this heavenly sun. He himself, like a second S. Francis about to write his rule, betook himself into the remotest part of the house, where he spent three weeks in solitude, silence, prayer, fasting, wearing hair-shirts, and using other macerations of the flesh, and writing those holy Constitutions which the Holy See has since approved and which nearly the entire Order has received with admirable increase of discipline.

It is the duty of everyone of us to consider what mode of life this truly apostolic man adopted and carried out during Lent. In a wonderful way he united action with prayer and mortification. He gave himself to study until eight o'clock. Then he repeatedly alternated prayer and the discipline,—the former that he might be enlightened by the divine light and that he might explain more clearly to the people the truths of the Gospel; the latter that while he was seeking to save the souls of others, he might not seem to neglect his own and that he might say with St. Paul, "I chastise my body and bring it into subjection lest when I have preached to others, I myself become a castaway."

We must not, therefore, think that prayer and contemplation must be reduced as much as possible in order that our apostolic labors may be increased. In fact, the greater things the Order essays to accomplish the more must it promote prayer and contemplation among its members, the more provide the accurate observance of these points which the Constitution prescribe for each and every one in this regard, the more it must courageously oppose any relaxation in this matter. Relaxation of this kind does not benefit but rather harms the apostolate.

Second. In undertaking external labors, it is proper that the Order itself and the individual religious be moved by a good intention.

Fr. Michael of St. Augustine numbers the good intention among the means by which the active life can be reconciled with the contemplative life without doing harm. "He who plans to erect the tower of perfection," he says, "must always have at hand a plumb-line by which to regulate all his works. Do you wish to know what this plumb-line is? Nothing else than the good intention by which we strive to please God alone, to avoid our own praise and satisfaction and all self-interest, to shut out completely all self-seeking even in God's gifts, and in all and through all things to aim at God's own pleasure and glory. Moreover, this most perfect intention must precede, accompany and follow all we do, since it is necessary by means of this plumb-line to regulate our whole life with the rule of perfection. Do not try to convince yourself that this or that work does not agree with your vocation; everything done in love and obedience and with a good intention for God, agrees excellently with your vocation."

These words are easily clear to all. Still it is necessary that not only individual religious but the whole Order must follow this rule. The Order, in making new foundations and in undertaking individual projects and labors, must seek not so much its own glory as the glory of God and the advantage of the Church. The more humbly it strives to serve the Church so much more glory and blessing will it find with God. Nor may we forget that a faithful and conscientious observance of regular discipline is the foremost service of God and the Church. Not without reason the Constitutions say, "Superiors should likewise provide that their subjects should render service both within and without our own churches and public oratories without, however, destroying religious discipline."

Religious discipline not infrequently collapses not because labors that have been undertaken are a hindrance, but rather because the religious themselves try to avoid religious discipline under the pretext of such labors. If we are animated with a good will and actuated by a good intention we can reconcile many things.

The monastery should offer an example and an occasion of regular life to those returning from external labors.

Third. In order that the mind may not be dissipated by external work, and that the love for prayer may not grow cold, our religious should accustom themselves to the practice of the presence of God.

Again our Fr. Michael of St. Augustine teaches, "It may likewise be said that the mortar by which all our works are joined in God, is the practice of the divine presence. If we always remember it when taking our meals and in doing our other duties of necessity, charity and obedience, it will tie together and direct all these to our chief end, viz., assiduous meditation on God's law and occupation of the soul with God."

If the practice of God's presence was necessary for our fathers who were contemplatives, because they could not apply their minds always to meditation proper and were detained by other just and necessary occupations, it is much more necessary for us who have gone over to the apostolic life and who are allowed to busy ourselves with God exclusively for only a short time. By this practice we guard against our going to our labors with a bad or imperfect intention and against permitting anything to be lost from our holocaust.

Fr. Michael de la Fuente always prayed, whether he was silent or whether he spoke, whether he ate or drank, studied or preached. Not merely occasionally but most frequently, and sometimes even when preaching, he sent forth ardent sighs from the burning furnace of his heart.

Without this practice of God's presence the saints would never have persevered so constantly nor worked so successfully. By this practice they were not only not estranged from attention to God while they were occupied externally, but they made greater and greater progress in union with God and in the fervor of religious discipline. External occupations do not of their own nature and of necessity draw away from God, but because we perform them distractedly and without a good intention. Per se when we hear confessions and assist the sick and dying, we come to know human life and misery better and more deeply, and being drawn away from the world we learn to love religious life and union with God more profoundly. The active life, likewise, rightly undertaken, contributes much to necessary mortification and consequently to a perfect union with God. The active life with proper safeguards creates occasions of a wide mortification and compels us to renounce our passions and inclinations in order that purity of heart and divine love may wonderfully increase in us. What influence life will exercise on us depends to a great extent upon ourselves, so that here also we may say, "Quidquid recipitur, recipitur per modum recipientis." "Whatever is assimilated, is measured by the capacity of the recipient."

Fourth. All matters should be governed by obedience.

Our Rule begins with obedience and prescribes that one of the religious should be elected Prior and that the rest of the religious should promise him obedience and should strive to render it in truth and reality. Of so great importance was obedience at the time when our life was eremitical.

Most appropriately the celebrated John Baptist Rossi admonishes his brethren, "You must all know that obedience is the foundation of your profession. Should you spurn it, your edifice will not only not rise in the Lord, but rather it will be destroyed and rooted up from the foundations."

For the same reason our Rule commands that the Prior should be the first to meet visitors to the monastery so that afterwards all that is to be done should proceed according to his decision and arrangement.

If in those days when the religious lived separated not only from the world but also more or less from the other brethren, and when all followed a very simple schedule of the day, if at that time I say, obedience was held to be the foundation of religious life, how much more in these times since we have been called to the active life. The greater dangers and labors an army has to overcome, the more severe the discipline to be observed and the more promptly and exactly must each one obey the commander-in-chief. "Every kingdom divided against itself, shall fall."

Besides, as we have heard, it is necessary that each and everyone should fulfill God's will and be led by a perfect intention in every undertaking. Now the divine will is not recognized more surely than by obedience, nor is the good intention strengthened more, than by obedience strictly observed in all things. For this reason Fr. Michael of St. Augustine says, "Every work done out of obedience in charity and God, agrees well with your vocation."

Where obedience fails, order fails, blessing fails. Not only does religious life collapse in the convent when the common exercises are neglected and despised but even many external apostolic labors are impeded. When efforts are not united by obedience and each one is led by his own inclination, it not rarely happens that the Superior has no one to hold sermons, to hear confessions and to visit the sick according to art. 187 of our Constitutions, even though these Constitutions expressly enjoin that no one should dare undertake anything inside or outside the monastery, such as hearing confessions, preaching sermons, and the like, without the express permission of the Superior. It is his duty to see that the religious are not kept outside the convent too long by outside work, and that they do not become unaccustomed to regular and common life.

When external activity is not strictly regulated by obedience, so that each religious chooses his labors, rather than is sent to them, quite frequently human motives creep in. Yes, it can happen, that some will neglect poverty and will labor more for the sake of gain than for the glory of God and the good of souls.

No one will deny that regular and spiritual life will be destroyed by such activity and that such zeal is only a sham. Active life of this type is not a source of glory but of disgrace to the Order.

Fifth. Work within the Convent and for the good of the Community should not be neglected or despised.

Although the Lord burned with great zeal for souls, He obeyed his Father's will and confined Himself within the limits of Israel, affirming to the Canaanitish woman that he did not wish to give to others the bread due the children. "It is not good to take the bread of the children, and to cast it to the dogs." It is not lawful, therefore, to take such care of seculars that neither time or strength is left to provide for the welfare of one's own religious brethren or only enough to fill them with the crumbs which fall from the tables of others.

Labors and undertakings which prevent Superiors from holding culpa regularly and caring for the affairs of their Convent, undertakings which prevent the appointment of a prefect for the professed clerics according to the prescriptions of the canons and which prevent the brothers and servants from obtaining the proper direction and catechetical instruction, are not an asset, but a liability to the Order and cannot be excused under the plea of zeal. Let us not forget the advice of St. Paul, "If a man have not care of his own, and especially of those of his house, he hath denied the faith, and is worse than an infidel."

If we act contrariwise, we do not bring any advantage to the Church either, since we may be compelled to entrust the care of souls, pulpits and confessionals to those who have not sufficiently acquired either profane or spiritual knowledge. Both shepherds and flock are exposed to the greatest dangers. We do not hesitate to affirm that if certain orders and religious Congregations much younger than we reap more and greater fruit in God's vineyard, it is due to the fact that these Orders take greater care of their religious, give them more time, and make a greater effort that their members may not only rightly and thoroughly accomplish their studies, but also drink in more deeply the spirit of their institute and implant solid virtues in their souls. Nor may we say that we are compelled by poverty to apply ourselves more frequently to outside works and to send our younger religious out earlier, since ordinarily the blessing of God is not lacking to religious striving after the religious and regular life. In fact it happens frequently if the interior life is neglected or slighted out of an excessive solicitude for earthly things, that through the imprudence and rashness of some religious who always had the appearance of zeal, we lose even those things which we have had for a long time. To religious also God has said, "Seek ye therefore first the kingdom of God, and his justice, and all these things shall be added unto you."

Let us, therefore, envy not only the number and renown of other religious, but also the "charismata meliora," the better gifts from which the former usually flow. And local Superiors should consider the wish of art. 313, "The Prior may not leave the place of his residence without serious and just cause which he should at once make known to the Provincial and then follow his orders."

Once more we must say that labors and works which can be done for the good of the Order in the solitude of monastery and cell, viz., the study and composition of books, should not be esteemed lightly.

Many indeed are most eager to apply themselves to preaching, hearing confessions and teaching externs, and they spare neither time nor strength; but when they meet enforced idleness they do not know what to do and are afflicted with an indefinable weariness, although being gifted with more than ordinary talents and faculties they could easily write books useful for religious and seculars, or work in the archives or in the library. They should take as their example the famous Fr. Marianus Ventimiglia at one time General of the Order and the composer of the book entitled "A Chronological History of the Latin Priors General of the Order of Our Lady of Mount Carmel." In the Preface of this book he confesses as follows: "Through the singular blessing of Almighty God, I have just been relieved of those most annoying cares that held me at Rome, and have been called to the former quiet of my little cell, to look after my own interests. In order that I might not without paying for it eat the bread which my Order so kindly provides, and in order to comply with our Rule, as is only just, which commands all to do some work that the devil may find us occupied, I decided to write this little volume in my spare time."

In this way all will love and observe the silence and solitude of their cells and will not yearn inordinately for external things; but they will not on this account be less ready or less fit when holy obedience calls them to external occupations. Lack of occupation has misled many to go out and to visit seculars too frequently, only to abuse their own time and others' time in useless, and even harmful conversations. On the other hand if we follow these counsels, we can exercise the most fruitful apostolate. For words pass; but writings remain and reach many. And besides, labors hidden within the convent and such as are never known to men, will be rewarded by God who sees all.

Let each one therefore zealously contribute to the good of the Order according to the talents granted him by God.

This activity which we have explained will inflict no harm on the interior life or on religious discipline. Rather, just as activity draws from them its strength and blessing, so through it, they will be more loved and more cultivated. For no one will experience more forcibly how necessary are prayer and the raising of the mind to God, than he who led on by zeal strives to win souls for God. From day to day he will persuade himself more and more that without God he can do nothing at all; he will not be satisfied with taking refuge in continual prayer, in as far as he can and may do so, but he will also try to strengthen his prayers after the manner of the Saints by mortification and self-denial. "The prayer of him who humbles himself, will pierce the clouds."

Sixth. It is well to remember, too, that the apostolate within the convent can and must be frequently exercised by prayer and mortifications offered to God for the conversion of sinners and the salvation of souls. Thus did our Saints, and notably St. Theresa of Jesus who wished to immolate herself for the conversion of heretics; St. Therese of the Child Jesus, who always prayed and made sacrifices for the missions, and so merited to be named the Patron of Missions; Mary Magdalen de Pazzi whose charity toward her neighbor and zeal for souls were so great. "Therefore she freely spent the powers of soul and body to help him corporally and spiritually and all to such a degree that for him she wished to be deprived of every comfort and was ready to undergo every suffering. In fact, in order that she might decrease the number of souls in sin, she would take terrible disciplines in the darkness of midnight; then she would gird herself with a belt studded with points; again she would hide herself to pray in hidden corners of the monastery; then she would plead with the divine Majesty to pierce the hardened hearts of sinners with the sweet arrow of His love and turn them to penance. Especially in the days before Ash-Wednesday, when the good God is more often offended, she would double her usual exercises and spend the entire night in tears and sighs."

We can therefore always work for the salvation of souls outside and inside the convent. Only one thing remains. Inflamed with holy love and directed by holy obedience we must execute what the divine will seems to demand of us at every moment. So the examples of the Fathers teach us.

CHAPTER V

Devotion to Mary

THE DOUBLE spirit of Carmel, i.e., the contemplative and active, is thrown into bolder relief and brought to greater perfection by a singular devotion to the Blessed Virgin.

We do not wish to demonstrate the self-evident and it would be an insult to try to prove this to a Carmelite, inasmuch as the Order is called by excellence the Order of the Brothers of the Blessed Virgin Mary of Mount Carmel and all of us have bound ourselves by profession made explicitly also to Our Lady. No one, therefore, possesses the spirit of Carmel in its perfection unless he burns with the highest love for this dearest Mother who has wrought so many benefits, signs and miracles for our protection, and unless he strives to propagate with all his strength her glory and devotion.

It is a somewhat difficult and rather delicate question to point out the particular note of Carmelite devotion to Mary by which it is distinguished from the devotion of others. As far as we ourselves are concerned, we believe that there is no reason to ask such a question, and that it can hardly be answered, because devotion to Mary, like Christian perfection, is one. All depends on the peculiar temperament of the individual client of Mary and on the direction of the Holy Spirit. The more we attempt to define and divide the spiritual life, the more difficult we make it.

Although it is necessary to have certain laws for living in each religious Order, and also some special spiritual direction adapted to and in agreement with the special end of each, still great liberty must be granted to the interior life of individual members so that grace may be cultivated rather than suppressed. Let us not be too anxious to distinguish ourselves from other orders in matters of detail. As for a difference, moreover, we seem to be distinguished from others quite sufficiently by the Scapular itself.

In general, it quite suffices to excel in fervor and zeal. Thus on our present subject it will be possible to give only a few counsels by the observance of which devotion to Mary cannot help flourish among us as befits Carmelites.

Before all we must by our love toward Mary, strive to have the Order fully and perfectly correspond to what we have explained in the foregoing sections that in this way it may excel others by religious observance. If our Order is honored and distinguished by Mary's name and patronage, so that it is called eminently Marian, without doubt whatever renown or infamy is found amongst us, redounds to the renown or disgrace of our heavenly Mother and Patroness. Wherefore, we are really sons of the B. Virgin Mary of Mt. Carmel, if we lead a truly Carmelite life and in due proportion add the active life to the life we choose to call our chief aim. We must never lose sight of this foundation and proof of our love and devotion for Mary. The principle before us must be that of St. Andrew Corsini, "Since I belong to thee, O Virgin Mary, I will generously serve thee day and night; but pray to thy Son that He may graciously pardon the sins of my youth. In proportion as I have displeased Him and thee by my evil life, I will try to please you both with all my strength by changing my life." And he besought the Bl. Virgin Mary that God might change his cruel and wolf-like nature, so "that," as he said, "by faithfully serving thee out of love for thy Son, I may become a meek lamb in thy Order and worthy of the sacrifice of praise."

The most intense and persevering striving for

religious perfection after the manner of the holy fathers, and the prescriptions of our Rule! Behold the first and fundamental means to honor Our Lady! The Mother is rejoiced at the holiness of her children; but she does not regard exterior service so much as interior, since only through perfection will we be able to praise God and to be happy forever in her company.

It is the duty of Carmelites to strive courageously and strenuously after perfection by following the Bl. Virgin Mary as their leader and teacher. After our Lord no one will incite us more to virtue than she. In the Bl. Virgin Mary we shall find all Carmelite virtues most perfectly displayed; a burning love for prayer and contemplation, unceasing union and conversation with God, love of silence and solitude, an absolute spurning and renouncing of creatures, prompt obedience and resignation to God's will, a most fervent charity toward all men, which magnanimously offered up everything for their salvation, sparing not even the sharpest sufferings.

Therefore, frequent recourse to the Bl. Virgin and meditation on her virtues will imbue us more from day to day with the true spirit of Carmel.

Such devotion to the Bl. Virgin will be no obstacle to our ascending to the highest degrees of the mystical life by means of contemplation, if God so wishes. Indeed the Ven. John of St. Samson testifies that God Himself is perfectly portrayed by the Bl. Virgin and that His perfections are found in hers. The Lord and His beloved Mother are filled with one and the same spirit.

How appropriately John Andrew de Pignariis, Provincial of the Holy Land who wrote the Acts of the General Chapters held in 1434 and 1440, prefaced them with the invocation, "Jesus in corde, Maria in mente!"

Again our Fr. Michael of St. Augustine teaches

us, "Therefore those who profess to be her well-beloved sons use that same discerning eye by which to discover whether that which they are doing or omitting is according to God's pleasure and that of His loving mother. They strive in all their deeds and omissions to have an eye turned to God and His most holy Mother so that they promptly and cheerfully may execute what they know pleases God and Mary, and sedulously avoid what they know displeases them." All blessings are to be looked for from divine grace which flows to us through the hands of Mary.

In fact he admonishes us to live, to work, to suffer, to die not only in God, but also in Mary; not only for God, but also for Mary. He seems to agree more or less with the "True Devotion to Mary," taught by Bl. Grignon de Montfort. However, Fr. Michael of St. Augustine is the older.

The doctrine found in the "Methodus Orandi" seems to be more easily understood and practiced: "We are taught by the tradition of the fathers and by the example of the saints of our Order, to offer to God every thing we do through the hands of His most holy Mother. See how the true devotion of a Carmelite comes from her or proceeds through her hands."

To depend absolutely on our most loving Mother, to confide in her to the limit of our powers, to do all and to suffer all in her honor, to be ready for everything in her honor, to stand with her at the side of Christ's cross! Behold the genuine Carmelite devotion to Mary!

If we are animated and inflamed by such love, we will practice everything else; we will not neglect outward demonstrations of love and devotion or pious exercises in her honor. As Carmelites we will always carry the Scapular with joy and love; we will say the Rosary daily according to the mind of the Church and the wish of our Constitutions. We will not be surpassed in the exercises of piety which seculars are wont to perform in honor of Our Lady, though prudence dictates not to crush the interior devotion and spirit by a multitude of external exercises nor to reduce unduly the time intended for meditation and contemplation. For our first duty toward our Bl. Mother is to observe faithfully all that the spirit of Carmel requires and our Rule and Constitutions prescribe.

Now since we have passed to the active or apostolic life, what more befits us Carmelites than to propagate as much as possible devotion to Our Lady among the faithful? To do this the individual Convents should exactly observe the requirements of Chapter One of our Constitutions. Moreover, every religious should edify seculars in word and deed in honor of the Blessed Virgin, to whom we are especially bound and we should sing the praises of our heavenly Mother as much as we can. In order to be able to do this rightly, let us not forget to apply ourselves to the study of Mariology according to art. 214.

The Bl. Virgin herself has placed the best means in our hands when she presented us with the Scapular.

Let us so much more readily and fervently employ all these means as both faith and experience teach us that souls are most easily brought to lead a Christian life, yes, even to attain perfection by devotion to Our Lady. We should recall that we have made our profession, "to God and to the Bl. Virgin Mary of Mount Carmel."

Again the more vehemently we burn with love for Mary, the more perfectly we will acquit ourselves of our other obligations, the more perfectly we will lead the Carmelite life, the more will our Order flourish inwardly and outwardly. All good things come to us together with her, and innumerable riches through her hands.

Conclusion

The truly Carmelite life is composed of three elements: Occupation with God, zeal for souls, singular love for the Bl. Virgin.

Occupation with God forms the foundation or principle upon which all else rests; the cornerstone, the removal or destruction of which will entail the collapse of the entire edifice.

Zeal for souls is the precious fruit derived from occupation with God or from contemplation. For by contemplation our soul is set afire with such a love of God, that we determine not only to save our own souls and to immolate ourselves completely to Him but also to gain other souls for God and to spare neither labor nor suffering in doing so.

Our singular love for Our Lady throws a characteristic light upon both these elements, brings strength and perseverance and obtains for us the blessing of Heaven. And even when we are occupied with God, we contemplate the Blessed Virgin in whom God's perfection shines forth as in a mirror, so that by devotion to Mary we arrive at a better knowledge of God; and when we work hard for souls we are not unmindful to spread Mary's honor, and we can hope to obtain the choicest success through her and with her.

Behold how these three characteristics harmonize, interpenetrate and assist one the other, so that the three really constitute a living and organic whole and no Carmelite will have to strain himself unduly to be faithful to his state and to our spirit in all three points. If all three are rightly and fully understood, we will not injure the others, nor will one be neglected or slighted on account of the others. In fact each is perfected and safeguarded by the others. A man who is truly a Carmelite, is truly perfect.

PART TWO

What We Must Do to Attain the Perfect Carmelite Life

CHAPTER I

The Duties of the Novice-Master

AFTER OUR exposition of what constitutes the truly Carmelite life, the question arises how to establish and develop this life in the Order. Before all things there comes to our mind the office of Novice-master since it is he who must give our members their first information, and whether they receive a correct idea of Carmelite life, depends without doubt on his effort and labor. For this reason we must treat in a special way of the office of Novice-master.

It is, therefore, the duty of the Novice-master to have the novices entrusted to his care imbibe the truly Carmelite spirit, and to see that the novices not only profess this Carmelite life in due time but also that they faithfully continue in it.

Since the Novice-master is seriously obliged to employ all diligence that the novices are sedulously exercised in religious discipline according to the Constitutions, let him not be ignorant of what he must do. Since, moreover, both the teachings of our ancestors, as well as experience have taught us that the relaxation of religious discipline rises chiefly from excessive ease in receiving aspirants into the novitiate or in excessive difficulty in expelling novices and also from carelessness in educating and training them holily, it is evident that in a sense the fate of the whole Province is in the hands of the novice-master. How correctly, therefore, the Constitutions of Tours say, "How important the office of the Novice-master is, is clear from the mere fact that to him is entrusted the education of those through whom the Order is to be preserved and propagated."

SECTION ONE

The Novice-Master Must Set the Example

"THE FIRST incentive to learning is the excellence of the master," says St. Ambrose. Wherefore the Novice-master must first of all display in himself the ideal according to which he expects to train his novices. Therefore besides the fact that according to Canon Law and the Constitutions he must be thirty-five years old and ten years professed, he must also be endowed with those qualities without which the instruction and training of the novices is practically impossible.

He himself should be, as far as possible, a true and perfect Carmelite as we have described him, so that before he tries to teach in words, he must display his doctrine by his example. The Constitutions of Tours require, "that he should be endowed with sufficient learning; be assiduous in the practice of prayer and mortification; dignified yet affable; burning with the zeal of God, yet tempered with discretion and kindness; as far as is possible free from every disturbance of mind and movement of affection, so that he may always edify his novices by word and example."

It is in every way necessary that the Carmelite Novice-master be in the highest degree attached to prayer, and consequently also to silence, solitude, and internal conversation with God, so that he may sincerely and persuasively attract his novices to them and he should excel in experience wide enough to direct the novices in such matters. Without fire we cannot inflame others. He who prefers labor outside the Convent with seculars rather than solitude, silence and conversation with God, will not give himself entirely to his novices. Nor is he fit to teach others abnegation and mortification, who has not experienced its fruits and possibilities, particularly since the very office of Novice-master, provided it is faithfully discharged, demands not a mere modicum of self-denial. Moreover, he will not make any progress without constantly asking God's blessing by prayer and mortification.

Only a truly spiritual man, dead to himself and living in God, seems fit to be called to so great and sublime an office.

It is evident at once that this proposition must be considered by those whose duty it is to elect the Master. Likewise it must be continuously and thoroughly considered by the one who is elected. For he must strive and strain to acquire what is lacking in himself, and to perfect what is imperfect, so that when he is urging others to run the way of perfection, he may run before and from day to day fulfill his duty more perfectly. Therefore he must not only apply himself to his spiritual exercises and to the presence of God as becomes a Carmelite, but he must also unweariedly read spiritual books so that he may draw also from the experience of others and become acquainted with the whole of spiritual life. For it is not lawful to limit the spiritual life by this or that secondary circumstance and so rather to hinder than to fortify the way to perfection. Moreover, the spiritual life is of such vast expanse, that no one can of his own experience be equal to every situation. There is danger of painting the spiritual life according to one's own inclinations, and then trying to fashion and instruct everyone according to this quite narrow idea, without considering the character of the individual and the will of the Holy Spirit.

Particularly should the Novice-master prefer the books of our writers, not despising or neglecting the rest, as also Commentaries on our Rule, so that in this way he may understand and assimilate Carmelite spirituality. We should calmly meditate on those things which our fathers have taught and done, so that we may be called, and indeed be, their sons. It is necessary to be familiar with Carmelite tradition in order to pass it intact to posterity. There is great danger of neglecting our tradition and of changing the spirit of the Order according to one's own taste and of distorting it only too promptly for modern purposes. This danger can be avoided only by reading and understanding what our predecessors and fathers have thought and written.

For the same reason the Master will give attention to the history of the Order. In this way he himself will burn with a love for the Order and he will bring others to burn with the same love.

He will likewise forestall discouragement of soul on account of these our critical times, and he will work with all his power that our glorious history will be repeated; he will work by instructing and educating our novices well.

The Novice-master must also burn with zeal for souls not only of those God entrusted to him, but also of seculars. Since the spirit of the Order is a double one, it is not right for the Master to cultivate only one in himself and in the novices. The Constitutions of Tours say, "Although one thing is especially necessary before all else, namely to occupy ourselves with God, the Novice-master will recommend all the external exercises of our holy Order to his novices, and show them how they are to be performed in the spirit of God. Likewise he will remember to explain frequently that all the duties of our Order must be held in equal esteem and must be undertaken out of eager obedience. Let him, however, carefully beware of turning their minds away from other occupations of our holy Institute under the pretext of recollection; and on the other hand of dissipating and extinguishing the interior spirit under pretext of adaptability for externals. Rather let him strive to imprint deeply in their minds the union and fusion of the double spirit of our Fathers Elias and Eliseus."

For this reason the Novice-master must leave nothing undone to have the novices imbibe this double spirit in due proportion, and to have them become fit to labor fervently in their turn for the salvation of souls. He must, moreover, pour out his prayers and offer the sacrifices demanded by his office as well as other voluntary mortifications to God for souls and he should have the novices do likewise. For the novices will gladly and faithfully do everything in the novitiate; they will give themselves promptly to prayer and suffering mortifications, when they find out that these will also help souls and when they have been taught that prayer and the pursuit of their own perfection is the foundation of the true apostolate.

When St. Mary Magdalen discovered a sister given to melancholy, she would scold her, saying, "You do not love God. Else why are you sad? You would do better by thinking of saving someone's soul and how you can free him from the clutches of the demon and gain him for God." Then she would teach her to say some little prayer, adding, "Courage because you will obtain it. For one of the reasons why God has drawn us from the world is that we may assist the Church to convert sinners." She used to say to her novices, "If you were able to behold the beauty of one soul in the state of grace, you would be taken with such a love for it that you would be unable to ask anything else of God. On the other hand, if you were to behold a soul in mortal sin, you would immediately burst into tears and you would abominate sin more than you would the devil himself, and you would always pray for the conversion of sinners."

Moreover the Master should delight to live among the young and to converse with them; neither should he lack the knowledge of psychology as it is called or of human nature so that he may know not merely how to explain his doctrine in a general way, but also how to give correct advice adapted to the individual to direct him in the way of salvation and perfection. For many are gifted with quite extensive knowledge and yet do not know how to apply it. Inasmuch as such knowledge is a gift of God, it must frequently be asked of the Holy Spirit and then be increased by observation of one's own self and of others. How shall he who does not know himself appraise others? Love will make him penetrate the character of youth more deeply, will discover helps and hindrances, and will not be deceived by mere form, or flattery or pretense. If the Master does not love his office and his novices with a truly supernatural love, he will hardly make any progress in training his candidates. He should frequently consider how great treasures are entrusted to him and with what responsibility he is burdened in order not to omit a thing in properly fulfilling his office.

SECTION TWO

The Novice-Master Must Teach

THE NOVICE-MASTER will strive to present a sound doctrine to his novices so that when they set out to correspond to their religious vocation they may not be ignorant of what they must do and omit.

They must know in what perfection itself consists for the acquisition of which they have entered the

Order. Perfection in its entirety is to be explained; but ignorant of essentials, the novices may indulge in singularities. It is clear to everyone that the greatest harm can come from such singularities not only to individual religious but also to communities themselves.

Still it is not lawful to brand the fervent pursuit of perfection with the mark of singularity, nor are they who with prudence do works of supererogation after the intention of our Rule, to be accused of singularity. Oh that all were so fervent that they should need restraint rather than encouragement! Indeed the Novice-master should frequently warn the novices that they have by no means satisfied their vocation if observing only the external requirements of the law, they have neglected to root out vice and to implant virtue, and that they will never become true Carmelites if they give themselves over to external labors and neglect to practice the interior life. He should teach them that all depends upon the assiduous, brave, and constant employment of self-denial and mortification and not upon sweetness experienced during prayer; and that no one will ascend to higher things unless he has presented God a heart free from every sin and dead to itself. If the novices are convinced of these truths, they will when the novitiate is over set out on the right way,—an aim for which the Master must strive with all his strength.

Then it is self-evident that the novices must be taught the means for arriving at perfection, i.e., prayer, the fruitful reception of the Sacraments, both general and particular examination of conscience, spiritual reading, the conquering of temptations, the acquisition of virtues, etc. Because he who wishes to acquire some art, must also know the necessary instruments and how to use them. The Novice-master must not only speak of obligations but he must also clearly demonstrate the fruits to be derived from perfection, so that the novices will be incited to the pursuit of perfection not so much by fear as by joy and desire. Let him stir up in them a filial love toward God the Father, and a tender affection toward our Divine Redeemer who has suffered so much for us; let him point out that notwithstanding the sacrifices required for perfection, no one except a perfect man will enjoy the perfect peace of Christ surpassing all understanding, and that therefore only he can be called happy, whereas the man who indulges himself is blown about by every wind. Let the Novice-master warn the novices time and again that it is better to go back to the world, than to live imperfectly and negligently in the religious state, and that the beginning must be made seriously and now, because later they will never make it.

After these preliminaries the Master will explain in what the essence and purpose of our Order consists. This will not be difficult for one who has himself been animated long since by the true spirit of Carmel. We have already shown how even in the novitiate the double spirit of our Order can be put in practice. It will be more difficult not merely to teach the novices, but to incite them to desire and as far as possible to strive to be thoroughly penetrated by that spirit.

For this purpose the Master will untiringly implore divine grace for himself and for his novices; but especially must he unfold before their eyes the glorious deeds and examples of our forefathers and of the Saints of our Order, and how widely the Order spread under the special protection of the Blessed Virgin when the true Carmelite spirit flourished, and how much the Order has contributed with God's permission to the good of the Church and the salvation of souls.

He should very thoroughly teach them the glorious history of our Order entirely in conformity to truth. He should relate its vicissitudes, and point out their causes and roots, as far as can be done; he shoud treat the lives of the Saints of our Order; he should teach the names of our chief writers and of the Priors General; he should indicate the principal books written by our members, so that the novices may not be ignorant how much our religious have labored and thus may be allured to rivalry and imitation. He can advantageously employ pictures for this purpose. In this way, will the novices burn with the desire of bringing back the pristine splendor of the Order insofar as it can be done.

The Master, however, must not cease to remind them that external splendor and extensive growth are of no avail, unless religious life truly flourishes within the heart, in fact, that we can never hope to have the Order vigorous once more and recovering its pristine rank in the Church, unless the foundation of holiness has first been laid by the religious. Moreover, everything depends upon God's blessing of which all must try to make themselves worthy. Even novices can contribute their share to this growth when they seriously pursue the spiritual life according to the Rule and Constitutions.

In this way such a desire will not be lost in mere affections, but will bear the fruits of good works, and indeed permanent ones. When we imitate our holy fathers, we guard the interests of the Order; in this way, too, no one will ever lose heart, since no one, no matter with how little talent he is gifted or with what sickness afflicted, is hindered from working in this way for the good of the Order. Indeed godliness is profitable to all things.

The Master must teach the novices the Rule and he must show its depth and extent, lest deceived by its brevity they have little regard for it and pay attention only to the Constitutions. The novices must know that the Rule is still essential and that the Constitutions are appendices to it, derive their force from it and guarantee that it be observed in spirit and in truth. A proof is that the Constitutions order the Rule to be memorized. He will likewise explain how the Rule and Constitutions are related and how the Rule is clarified by the Constitutions so that the novices will be convinced that they cannot be called, much less be, true Carmelites, unless they observe them in detail. In them our entire perfection is contained.

S. Mary Magdalen de Pazzi was drawn by the greatest affection toward our holy Order. And if she ever saw the Order harmed in even the smallest way, she would immediately report it to the Superiors without any human respect. She frequently asked the older mothers of her monastery to use most watchful care over every rule of their holy Order. Because, she would say, if even the smallest of our holy Rules be broken, not so much the Order would be insulted, as the pupil of God's eye, inasmuch as the Order is the house of God and most dearly beloved by Him. Concerning the holy Rule she was accustomed to say that she would prefer to undergo every torment rather than behold even the tiniest order infringed. She also showed this in deed, whenever some common exercise of the monastery was to be performed, no matter how abject it was. For then this zealous Mother would be frequently awake at midnight to do it herself, so that the Sisters who had this charge, might satisfy the ordinary schedule of the house.

The Master must not be content to explain the Rule and Constitutions, but he must assure himself that the novices have understood everything well, particularly since the novitiate is the foundation and root of the religious life and novices usually follow the way they have learned in the novitiate. Therefore time is lost if the novitiate consists only in this, that the novices according to the prescriptions of the Canons are free from all other occupations, and like captives yearning for the beginning of their liberty await the end of the novitiate year.

For the Carmelite, instruction in the art of prayer and meditation is of greatest importance because it pertains to the chief aim and the foundation of Carmelite life. It is not sufficient, therefore, that the novices be imbued with the desire and love of prayer and meditation, but they must also be taught how to pray and how to progress in meditation. That is why the Master should repeatedly instruct them in the method of meditating and examining their conscience, in the various ways of praying and directing their actions together with the practice of God's presence, so that afterwards they may be lovers of the interior life and as far as God grants, observers of it according to the Rule.

If he has accomplished this, he has not labored in vain. If he has not, he must be convinced that he has lost time and labor. If the novices love and cultivate prayer and meditation, provided they have the right idea of prayer, they will make progress in virtue and when the novitiate is finished will not turn aside from the right path. Thus it will not be sufficient for the Master to explain in general how to pray and meditate, but he must treat individually and frequently in private with the novices about their difficulties.

Each morning St. Mary Magdalen de Pazzi proposed to her novices the points she wished them to consider during the day. If one did not know how to meditate, in order to teach her and accustom her to it, she would meditate with her, audibly expressing her own meditation.

Among the various methods the affective should be preferred, since this is properly Carmelite. Still the freedom of the individual should not be excessively curtailed, since neither limits nor obstacles should be placed to the grace of God from which everything depends in the matter of prayer. It is quite sufficient that each one goes forward in his own way and that the fruits of prayer are evident in his daily life.

It seems to be necessary, however, that each one must begin with some definite method, especially, if heretofore, he has not learned or practiced meditation. Gradually other methods can be explained so that each one can choose one suited to himself, although it is always necessary to follow a special attraction of the Holy Spirit.

For the rest it is most of all necessary sincerely to desire the gift of prayer. The divine help will not be lacking to those who will and persevere, provided not merely the delights of prayer are sought for and that self-denial and mortification are not neglected. All these must the Novice-master inculcate lest the novices desist from praying when difficulties arise.

The advantage and the necessity of solitude and silence for progress in prayer and meditation must frequently be held before the novices. Novices should be told to love and cultivate silence and solitude for the sake of prayer; they should strive by this very love of silence and solitude to be more ardent in prayer and meditation. If this condition is realized they will be prompt to set all self-love aside and to leave God for God's sake to take up whatever labors may be demanded by obedience, charity or necessity.

A careful and profound instruction concerning God's presence must not be omitted. By this practice, as we have explained, we fulfil the prescription of our Rule, we are emancipated from creatures, and when we have tasted heavenly delights we are drawn to still higher things. Thus our souls are prepared for the mystical state, if so be God's will. Without the practice of God's presence the spiritual life will hardly ever get beyond the stage of beginners.

A thorough examination of conscience is necessary to procure purity of heart. The more this practice is repugnant to nature, the more useful it is, inasmuch as it guards against illusions and strengthens the foundations of humility. St. Mary Magdalen de Pazzi wished her novices to make an examen of conscience three times a day.

The particular examen should be well and thoroughly explained; otherwise it can happen that religious will never know how to make it. The greatest difficulty in this regard seems to be the selection of a subject and its proper division. For this reason help must be given to the novices so that they may lose no time.

Moreover, the Constitutions say that the Novice-master should teach his novices fervently and devoutly to undertake penance for their past life. This penance is not satisfied by a general confession, but later on all the austerities and difficulties of religious life must be borne from the motive of penance, and voluntary mortifications must be discreetly added according to strength and temperament. The novices should be frequently reminded that Carmelites are called to do penance both for themselves and for others and that it is not sufficient to carry the name and habit of a religious, at the same time yearning for the conveniences of life more than seculars do. Yet they should be taught that penance is not gloomy or lacking joys, since penance and austerity of life pave the way for the peace of Christ which according to the Apostle surpasseth understanding and which the world can neither give nor take away. They should likewise be taught that our own concupiscences and passions are the greatest enemies of true peace and perfect joy. Unless we shall practice penance, our religion and our piety are vain.

To omit, in the instruction of novices, the doctrine of proper mortification and self-denial would be a crime, inasmuch as we progress only as we do violence to ourselves. Therefore the novices should acquire the discreet use of those instruments which from olden times have been used to chastise our body. Not even the Apostle, wearied as he was by his labors and exhausted by misfortunes and persecutions, omitted to chastise his body. A prudent Master will not hide from his novices that perfection is not comprised in these practices but when they are employed with common sense they are of great value.

It is highly important for the novices to conceive from the very beginning a right idea of their relations with their own family, their parents and relatives. It is necessary to convince them that they cannot be true and perfect religious unless they free themselves from every inordinate attachment to their relations. Likewise that from now on they must look after the salvation of their own souls and the good of the Order, leaving all care of their family to God who will provide for their relatives in proportion as the novices dedicate themselves to His service. Therefore they should frequently pray for their own, but they should never be unfaithful in any way to their obligations on account of their relatives, since "No man putting his hand to the plough, and looking back, is fit for the kingdom of God." In order to become accustomed to all this the novices should not be allowed to write letters too often or to receive visits. The parents, likewise, and also relatives should from the beginning be made to feel that the religious has ceased to be a member of his own family. Otherwise later on greater and more frequent difficulties will arise. Experience teaches!

With such a foundation it will be easy to stimulate the novices to a true zeal for souls by the example of our holy fathers Elias and Eliseus and of the other Saints of our Order.

When St. Mary Magdalen de Pazzi was mistress of the younger Sisters she strove to enkindle in her spiritual daughters the intense zeal for souls with which she herself burned. Thus she used to say to them, "Do you know that we should have to humiliate ourselves exceedingly, if through our negligence many souls have gone down to hell which now would be in eternal glory if we had been fervent in offering up for them the Blood of Christ?" This zeal, as we have suggested, the novices should begin to practice at once by means of prayers and sacrifices; in fact, they should include this intention in all the sacrifices of the novitiate so that they may prepare themselves to receive worthily one day the sacred priesthood, if God so wills it.

Our old Constitutions ordained the following: "The novices should be exercised for some time in all the duties of the household excepting those for which they are unfitted by age and strength and by which they might be too much distracted, such as is the office of receiving guests, of the common infirmary, of the porter, etc. These and similar offices they will not perform." It will not be out of place to have such duties in mind so that the novices may become fit for manual labor, and particularly that they may learn to combine properly the active and contemplative life, without, however, losing internal recollection of soul.

The Novice-master must not forget to teach the novices that politeness and etiquette are of the highest importance for the reputation of the Order and for the sacred ministry. Suitable rules should be given them, and they should be taught and compelled to observe exactly the points found in Chapters XVI and XVII of the Constitutions with reference to conduct inside and outside the monastery. In such practices, however, as shown above, there is found a splendid opportunity of mortification and self-denial. Hardly anyone will deny that in this way the souls of seculars are more easily attracted by a well-trained priest and religious and the floodgates of grace are opened to souls.

Not without reason do our Constitutions warn that our religious should discreetly and modestly treat with seculars by observing the rules of politeness and that human means, when necessary, must be prudently and religiously employed. The Ven. John of St. Samson himself teaches likewise.

Again our Constitutions say: "Let the Master recommend to his novices a solid and truly child-like devotion to the Blessed Virgin and her Scapular." If the Master has brought his novices to our Mother, their vocation seems to be assured. But he should warn them that according to what we explained above, they should strive to please the Blessed Virgin by diligently practicing a truly religious and Carmelite life and by striving with all their might to become true Carmelites. They should put everything in the hands of our Immaculate Mother, and they should do all for love of her. Finally the entire doctrine of the Church concerning Mary should be explained so that their devotion to Mary may not be established on mere feelings but on explicit faith in the dignity and power of the Mother of God, our special protectress.

Consequently a conference about Mary should be held often, at least once a week.

The Master must pay special attention that the novices become accustomed to recite the Divine Office "digne, attente ac devote." For according to the Rule it is of supreme importance for a Carmelite. The Constitutions explicitly ordain, "The Master will see that the clerics learn ecclesiastical chant and the Rubrics of the Ceremonial and they shall frequently submit to an examination in these matters. We also recommend the interpretation of the Psalms."

The novices should accustom themselves to observe minutely what is inculcated in Chapter XI concerning the Divine Office; especially, that they always be on time when the signal with the bell is given, that they respect the asterisks, that they distinctly and clearly utter each word and each syllable, that they recite on the same tone as the others, and that they perform the ceremonies, bows and genuflections as prescribed. Unless they have been introduced to these things as novices, they will never learn them.

St. Mary Magdalen de Pazzi was very anxious to have great skill in and affection for the proper recitation of the Office, because this is one of the chief obligations of nuns by which the Divine Majesty is recognized, honored and adored. Therefore before they went to choir she would call them aside and say to them, "My little children, remember that so far you have pursued human interests, in treating with creatures. Now you are going to an angelic function to treat with your Creator. This is of such importance that the blessed spirits whose purity is so admirable do not dare perform it without fear and trembling. How much more must we most unworthy creatures quail when we are about to appear before the sovereign Godhead. Therefore she wished that before the Office would start, they should elicit an act of humility, considering themselves unworthy to undertake an angel's duty. She taught them to offer these praises in union with those which the blessed spirits in heaven sing to God. Although our praises cannot ever attain the purity of those they offer God, we are not forbidden the desire of honoring Him in so sublime a manner. She very carefully watched how attentively the novices chanted in choir, how modestly they took part, with downcast eyes and the like.

We also read in the life of Fr. Philip Thibault, "The divine Office was rendered with such dignity of chant and splendor of ceremonies that on some feasts of the year sometimes twenty and even thirty members of the Breton council, both president and members, clothed in their official robes sat in our choir charmed more by the harmony of religious decorum which they saw shining forth in all of our religious than by the sweetest music with which the divine service was rendered in the cathedral and elsewhere."

Actual practice will help much toward this end. Gregorian chant is not to be slighted or neglected as the Constitutions expressly declare.

Before all, the novices should be taught the meaning of the divine Office and to love to recite in choir. Then they will enjoy every means to recite it well and will not try to be absent from choir for trivial reasons, a thing which the Master should never allow.

The liturgical training should be continued after the novitiate since it cannot be completed in the novitiate; still, unless a serious start is made in the novitiate, who will follow up? There is no intention to train our novices as theologians but to have them learn to recite the Office with fruit. Therefore the Master should sometimes, particularly before the great feasts, have the Office studied. Let him explain in a practical way, the difficult parts and demonstrate with what thoughts and affections it can be recited.

It will be useful to indicate to the novices certain apostolic intentions for each day or to have them pick their own according to their private devotion. They should be taught to have regard for their own affairs and necessities as well as those of the Church, of the Order and of their country. In this way they will better understand that the recitation of the Office is a public and very important duty and that when they recite it well they apply themselves to an affair of the highest importance.

Finally the novices should be taught how to correlate and unite their various exercises of piety so that one may support the other and a truly spiritual life may emerge. Because then the other occupations will be undertaken and accomplished in the same spirit of faith and piety.

The Master should employ every means to have the novices always desire most intensely to become perfect Carmelites and that each one by his life will desire and strive to contribute according to his power to the advancement and glory of the Order. A prudent and fervent Master will turn everything to the training and sanctification of his charges.

The Master is urged to carefully write out his teaching and to have the novices make a compendium of it. Thus they will have something afterward by which to recall the instruction of their Master and to help them to persevere in faithfully observing it.

The Novice-master should remember to illustrate and confirm his teachings with the examples and sayings of our own Saints.

SECTION THREE

The Master Must Train the Novices

THE MASTER is not merely obliged to present a certain spiritual doctrine to the novices, but he must also train them to live according to this doctrine. This matter should not be left to the novices themselves; but rather they must be induced and even in a certain sense compelled to do their duty. For the Master must help the novices to overcome both interior and exterior difficulties and then to live rightly and to acquire good habits. In a word, the novices are to be trained so that afterward they will live as Carmelites freely and without a monitor.

Beginners are usually animated with a good intention and an ardent zeal; yet, since they are beginners, they gradually meet quite serious difficulties, so that they grow faint, and unless they are supported, will hardly be kept on the right path. After these difficulties have been overcome, they very easily run the way of the Commandments and of the vows. The Master, therefore, is not merely a teacher of ascetical theology, but also a father and a leader in the spiritual life.

That is why, as we have already shown, the Master must take the lead by good example. A good example, we say, in all things even in outward bearing and in his way of speaking and acting. He should have drunk in deeply and should observe minutely all that our Constitutions prescribe about our conduct at home and outside. How will the novices learn the modesty and reserve enjoined there, if the Master himself violates these rules continually in word and deed and the novices suffer a great deal in this way?

He should no less carefully observe the order of the day, the ceremonies of the liturgy and the like.

The example of the Master is the first element of teaching as well as of training.

Still he should not be alone in doing these things but should provide with all love, fortitude and perseverance that the novices do them also. Nor should he slight or neglect the least faults committed by the novices. "He that contemneth small things, shall fall by little and little." Unless the Master makes note of every little thing, he will hardly help the novices. In a life circumscribed as the novitiate is, serious crimes and vices are hardly to be expected. But if such should occur, those guilty should be expelled, rather than trained, so that time and labor may not be wasted and others may not be infected.

The Master, therefore, should insist that they recite the Divine Office worthily and devoutly, that they come promptly to all community exercises, that they carefully observe solitude and silence, that they promptly and diligently perform the labors imposed on them, that they converse and associate quietly and kindly, that they listen to everything said to them. Let him never tolerate even the least disobedience.

In order that her novices might be zealous for holy obedience, St. Mary Magdalen de Pazzi employed anxious and watchful care. In fact, with this in view, she would often impose commands hardly in keeping with reason to see what they would do or answer. Thus when one was complaining to her that she could pray only with difficulty she would say, "Go out into the garden to that tree to learn from it and listen diligently what it has to say." The novice would immediately obey and it is not easy to describe how she afterwards felt herself incited to prayer, desiring to spend entire nights in it. To other novices she would say that they should put all confidence in obedience to obtain every heavenly gift. When sometimes she found them afflicted, she would say, "Why do you not throw all on obedience as though you were dead? Unless you do this, the service of God can never please you." She exhorted them also to offer their will as a sacrifice to God, promising them that they would draw thence great consolation. She would never allow them even only one or the other time to consider anything against obedience, because so, she said, they lost the merit of obedience, "If, however," she added, "you desire to fulfill the divine will, beware of drawing your Superior's will according to your own judgment; but always strive to execute his command in all simplicity; for thus you will arrive at great perfection." Again we read, "Toward two defects, she, otherwise most indulgent, showed herself rigid and unyielding and infallibly enjoined a severe penance for them, viz., if a novice said, I will or I will not; and if she spoke of others' defects, even the smallest."

The more important obedience is for the active life to which we have been transferred, so much more insistence must be placed on the novices' becoming accustomed from the very beginning to prompt obedience and the rejection of their own judgment.

With great love, prudence and patience the Master must from the beginning urge all we have explained; for unless a good beginning is made, there will be no success. Besides it is vain to defer until the morrow what must be done and taught this very day. Difficulties do not usually decrease in the course of time. In fact, novices seem to me more docile and flexible in the beginning, when their ardor still glows. The Master, therefore, should attack the beginnings; remedies may be applied too late when circumstances and evils have become worse. By prudence and love the novices should be elevated and assisted, but not overwhelmed.

Moreover, the Master should find out whether or not the novices practice what he teaches and counsels. He must have some assurance in this matter so that he may not run as at an uncertainty or as one beating the air. This will be accomplished by watchfulness.

The Master should not be misled into the expectation that all his words have fallen into the best ground and will bring fruit a hundredfold, without the necessity of his beating off the birds of prey of contrary inclinations, or without an enemy's planting cockle. Experience teaches far otherwise. If watchfulness should be neglected, the best novices can easily be held back by the others from doing all things perfectly, especially from religiously observing solitude and silence. But these excellent ones have the right to be assisted and defended by the Master in their efforts.

There are some, indeed, who are influenced by their own conscience and by the presence of God to perform everything faithfully and who need no one to watch them. Would that all were such! There are some likewise who in spite of the good will with which they are endowed, must on account of their inconsistency, levity or neglected training, be strengthened by the presence of the Master lest they fall. When these are accustomed to exact order they will gradually go forward so that they will guard themselves, particularly after they have become familiar with the practice of God's presence.

Then, too, it is impossible for the Master to judge rightly the character and qualities of each, and to direct them accordingly unless he watches attentively. The presumption that all are good and fitted for our Order must frequently yield to the truth. This truth will be recognized only by observation. By no means, however, do we advise the Master to act as a detective does in discovering crime.

He should do all things openly so that the novices may not be ignorant that the Master is on guard, and that he will see to it that they obey when he commands. Unless the Master acts thus the novices will easily conclude that he is indifferent in such matters.

Undoubtedly such vigilance canont be exercised by the Master without inconvenience and annoyance to himself. It is much easier to betake himself to his cell after he has held his lectures on the spiritual and religious life, not to worry about anything else, and to hope that all will act rightly and promptly execute what he has taught. But the Master like the Good Shepherd, will not avoid labors and inconveniences, in order to help the novices and to lead them to perfection. On the other hand, if he will suffer these labors, he will avoid others, since then it will not be necessary to repeat the same things again, and gradually the good seed will bear good fruit and at the end of the year he will not have labored in vain.

The Constitutions themselves enjoin, "Ordinarily the Master or his Socius, unless he is hindered, should be present at the acts at which the novices are present." For this will be necessary that the novices may not be subject to the influence of religious who may not be so good.

Our old Constitutions were much more explicit. "The Master should try to be in Choir and at the community exercises so that he may be able to observe the carriage and the actions of the novices." He should sedulously help them, particularly in the season of temptations and aridity. He should also try to visit them often so that they may the more easily give an account of their interior and exterior condition. He should provide for their necessities in a fatherly way. Nevertheless the Master must aim and plan to have them fulfill their obligations of their own free will. Again and again the novices should be warned that piety and exactness which proceed only from the fear and opinion of the Superior, are worth nothing. They should always and everywhere have God before their eyes who will be the judge of their actions.

It is a mistake to direct the training of religious in a general way to live according to their vows and to avoid violating the rules of the Order. This is not sufficient. The Master must strive to have the novices turn their sentiments and affections more and more from creatures and turn them to God. He should induce them to aspire sincerely to such abdication and with God's help to insure their arriving at it. Without this abdication they can never be disciples of the Lord and true religious.

Only in this way can their later religious life be placed in safety. If the novices have not understood the necessity of complete renunciation, their training has been nearly useless. Therefore, for example, St. Mary Magdalen de Pazzi stimulated her novices with most efficacious words to the observance of poverty, to despoiling themselves of the least possession. She frequently employed the words of that Saint who said, "Everything that is lacking to a religious in this life, will be returned to him a hundredfold in the next." She enjoined upon them to examine their conscience every day and to see whether they possessed even the tiniest thing to which they were inordinately attached; and that if they should find any such thing, they should immediately deprive themselves of it for the love of God. Thus when one of them brought her some prayer beads most pleasing to her, the Saint first deprived her of it; afterwards she returned it to her with the understanding that the novice was to return it to her every evening. By this means the novice made so much progress that she learned perfectly that she had nothing of her own but as borrowed from the Order. At another time she noticed a novice too much attached to a book in which she had entered some matters pertaining to her soul. In order to make her more pure before God, she ordered her to put it in the fire. "See! my little children, that you cannot remain long in the path of evangelical perfection, unless you have first learned to renounce your convenience a thousand times a day, because the entire occupation of the soul in this life consists in loving and hating; namely in loving God and hating self. In this is found our whole perfection."

And Fr. Philip Thibault like a true shepherd of Carmel drove his flock to the interior of the desert; I mean to the most intimate union with God, for the attainment of which he assigned various efficacious means; namely, an extraordinary purity of heart, forgetfulness of the world and worldly things, love of the cross, assiduous and unflagging zeal for overcoming one's self. Sometimes he gave them permission to humble themselves as much as they wished and of mortifying themselves with self-imposed sufferings so that in this way he might test their zeal, and also stimulate them, as it were, to adopt shortcuts to heroic sanctity. They in turn were not slow or cowardly to use this permission. Some of them attempted to confess their sins openly in the refectory with such humility and exhibition of repentance that they forced tears from those who heard them. But the prudent Superior bade them be silent, lest perhaps the weak derive as much harm as the former derived profit from their humility. Others performed penances with such zeal that they required to be checked. There were others who went about the dormitories in groups at dead of night, violently scourging themselves and in a mournful tone chanting verses from the Psalms of David. Lingering in the silence of night before the cells of the brethren, they very successfully incited their occupants to the love of God, a detestation of their sins and a zeal for penance.

But since mortifications inflicted by others touch more keenly than those inflicted by self he did not refrain from exercising and trying his novices with them. One splendid novice seemed to display a certain haughtiness in his countenance in his natural way of acting. Our Father ordered him to fetch water in a cracked jug from a public fountain outside the walls just at a time when the pupils and the masters of the Jesuit College were coming to our Church to attend divine services. The obedient novice did as he was told, and returned at the very hour, drenched from head to foot in the sight of all the students who had known him before, and loved and respected him on account of his remarkable talents. He dismissed another desirable novice from the foot of the altar where he was kneeling ready to pronounce his vows because he held some doubts about his constancy in the life of virtue just begun, so that he might first pay some debts which he had contracted through too free a life. The generous-hearted novice bore this refusal with undaunted spirit and having pronounced his vows on the following day became, just like the former novice, a great servant of God and one who rendered great service to his Order and the Province.

A prudent Master will understand what is proposed for admiration, and what for imitation, and will not despise the spirit just because he cannot follow the letter. So much however is clear. It is the Master's duty to try his novices by prudent and discreet practices, to discover and to cultivate the seeds of virtue, which may be found in them. This cannot be done by mere lectures; but it is necessary to employ timely practices to root out the seeds of vice, to check the emotions of the spirit and to acquire virtues. For this reason the Master has full power of trying and testing the novices both in the dining room and other places. For the same reason the old Constitutions read thus, "Besides the Conventual chapter of the Prior, the Master of novices should two or three times a week hear the faults of his subjects, correct their faults and impose penances and mortifications on them to be done publicly or privately."

In fact it seems proper that the novices should of their own accord accuse themselves of their faults to the Master and ask a penance.

For the novices must be trained!

SECTION FOUR

The Novice-Master Must Test His Novices

FINALLY the Novice-master having implored the light of the Holy Ghost, should try to know and understand his novices in such a way that he may give a correct judgment about their vocation. Although he must try to make them, as far as he can, fit for the Carmelite life, still he is allowed to propose only those for profession who are really fit. The Order itself expects the Master not merely to cherish and advance his plants with every care and foresight, but also to unearth and remove those that are evil and unfit. It is not the least advantage to the Order to aggregate to itself such candidates as are incapable to bear the burdens of Carmelite life and who are not called by God to our Order. It is God's office to call, not ours; and it is not lawful to do violence to the divine plans.

If in building anyone should employ timbers and stones which are unfit and not strong enough to bear their burdens, not only will those stones and timbers break and crumble in their turn, but the whole building will suffer damage.

Candidates without a vocation will sooner or later by word and example introduce relaxations; they will prevent the others from striving for perfection; by some scandal they will suddenly destroy what has been accomplished by the others with much labor; by their bad example they will turn away the regard of seculars from the whole community and will hinder others from desiring and asking the habit. Moreover they will diminish the blessing of heaven! Would that all who are concerned were convinced of this and would not allow themselves to be misled by a false love for unfit candidates and so act wrongfully toward the Order itself. Not without reason do the Constitutions say, "Long since, both the warnings of our ancestors as well as experience have taught us that the relaxation of religious discipline arises chiefly from too great a facility in receiving aspirants, or in too great difficulty in expelling them and from neglect to train them and teach them holily. It is evident, therefore, how necessary it is to watch over their reception and training."

Much to the point the Ven. John of S. Samson writes, "The reason why some Orders today are conducted more politically than spiritually is the large number of novices big and little of every kind and of every corrupt and vicious nature. Their bodies indeed are held within the cloister, clothed and fitted out with the religious habit, while their souls are gadding about the whole world. There is great danger that the Superiors as long as they continue to receive such unworthy novices, will afterwards suffer a terrific battle, a continuous martyrdom and great persecutions from these very novices. I for my part cannot see why they hesitate to reject those who are unfit for religious life. For by the fact that novices are indiscriminately received without testing their characters, evils are added to evils, and the old wounds are renewed."

Therefore the Novice-master cannot consent to profession, if a cleric gives no sure hope that he will be a truly religious man, a Carmelite and a priest according to the Sacred Heart of Jesus. He who cannot get along with others and lives in continuous disagreement with them; he who detests prayer, meditation and the Divine Office; he who cannot learn or can learn only with great difficulty the ceremonies of the choral recitation of the Office and of the serving of Mass; he who is not obedient and conducts himself disrespectfully to Superiors can hardly be received into the Order.

If it is evident that someone through lack of talents and character is not going to master the studies of Philosophy and Theology, he should be excluded from the vows, because the lips of the priest guard knowledge.

If bad morals are discovered in any novice, the Master must remove him from the others according to art. 49 of the Constitutions. But if any have lived evilly in the world, even though they have reformed, they should be received with caution and should be tested longer lest they fall into their former vices. We must not forget that illegitimate sons, even though legitimized, are invalidly accepted without an express dispensation of the Most Rev. Father General. Although they themselves must not be blamed for the sins of their parents, nevertheless, they not infrequently by reason of heredity or of defective training have a character that appears little fitted for religious life.

Bodily health must also be tested. If the Master notices that a novice does not rise promptly in the morning; that he is quickly tired by studies and other occupations, that he cannot sleep at night and is very nervous, that he does not eat most of the foods, that he is too fearful and anxious about his health, that he is suffering from some hereditary sickness, then the right conclusion is that he is not called to the religious life, since he is not equal to the corporal demands of religious life. Thus the Master cannot agree to his admission, since a sound mind must dwell in a sound body.

All these points hold more strongly concerning the lay-novices who are intended to do manual work in the Convent. If the Brother-novices show themselves unwilling or unable for corporal labors, they are much better kept out of the Order. The same holds good if they are too rough or rustic and cannot be changed or trained.

In order to find out all these points, the Master should not treat the novices with too much indulgence by exempting them more than necessary from community exercises or from their proper work. If the religious life should begin with dispensations, how will it end? If a novice is not equal to his obligations in the novitiate, how can we hope that he will be so later? The novice must accommodate himself to religious life, and not the religious life to the novice. Sometimes dispensations may have to be granted on account of youth, provided the good will and true religious spirit are evident. The Ven. John of S. Samson himself teaches this, though he believes candidates of too young an age or delicate a constitution should not be accepted.

If any doubts remain the Master should prudently strive to remove them by mortifications, penances and humiliations, so that from the reactions he can discover the true character and the true intention of the novice. For it is a question of greatest moment both for the candidates, who will not be satisfied without a vocation, as well as for the Order which will be drawn into serious danger by the reception of unworthy religious.

When candidates were received into the monastery for trial, St. Mary Magdalen considered attentively whether they were fit for the Order and how true and solid was their vocation. She would test and try them in various ways, and made known to them the entire routine of the monastery and the difficulties of religious life so that they would not be able to complain that they were ignorant of anything, or if they remained, be a burden or source of harm. When she found any reluctance in them she would say, "If our way of living does not please you, you can look for another place; we intend to keep the manner of life you see!' Although the good mother was full of compassion, she showed herself rigid and inflexible, and she was not influenced by any consideration of nobility, riches, or any other respect from saying her mind when there was question of religious observance. And she strove diligently to establish her daughters in true virtue, particularly that of mortification.

The office of Novice-master is not a light one, or an easy one, or one that can be entrusted to anyone. It is necessary to call to this office the very best, and it is not proper to relieve them without reason, inasmuch as they need long experience and in the beginning cannot know everything perfectly. Therefore the Constitutions say, "The Master of novices should be elected every three years and during his term should not be removed without a just and serious reason to be determined by the Provincial and the Definitors." And he can be re-elected without dispensation.

The old Constitutions explained this, "The Novice-master and his Socius should exercise this office three years and if they are fit, should continue. Because changing them will be not a little obstacle to uniformity in the education of novices."

Other conditions being equal, the best Master of novices is formed if one has filled the office of Socius for a number of years before being chosen Master.

It seems only proper that the Novice-master should make a longer retreat before assuming office.

We should not forget what both common law and our Constitutions order, "Both Master and Socius should be free from any duties and obligations which might hinder the care and the direction of the novices."

It is not fitting that the Novice-master be Prior or Procurator. The training of novices seems to be sufficiently important to engross the entire man, and is so sublime that the whole man should apply himself to it without division or distraction. There is no hope for the Order, if the training of novices is contemned. If the Order does not wish to spend anything in the training and educating of novices, it is neglecting itself and loses the right of admitting novices.

Therefore, if any Province is not capable of establishing a proper and well arranged novitiate, nothing else remains than that aspirants be sent to another Province. It is better not to have novices, than not to train them. In this way no remedy is applied to evils, but the evil is continued. One must not be deceived by the mere number of religious.

Those who by the grace of God desire our habit have the right to expect the opportunity and the possibility of learning a truly religious life, and that a Carmelite one, and afterward of living it to the end.

To despise or neglect vocations given us by God will make our account a difficult one before God's tribunal.

* * * * *

Although the primary and chief responsibility for the novices has been entrusted to the Novice-master, still he alone cannot sufficiently provide for the education and spiritual advancement of the novices, if the other religious do not lend their help, each one according to his duty and condition. In fact, the Master will labor in vain, if he is not helped by the others. Therefore, we now ask what the other religious, both Superiors and subjects, can and must do for the novitiate and for preserving the spirit of the novitiate.

CHAPTER II

The Duty of the Master of the Professed

THE PREFECT of the students or the Spiritual Director must continue and complete the task of the Novice-master. Our Constitutions prescribe thus, "A Prefect should be placed in charge of the professed students by the Provincial, whose duty it will be to exercise special care and directive power over them, even though they are priests, during the course of studies. He shall train their souls to the spiritual life by opportune advice, instructions and exhortations; he shall watch, moreover, that all the students entrusted to him remain separate from general association with the others, especially during recreation, and he shall see that they read these Constitutions several times."

"There is little use," say these same Constitutions, "for Religious Orders to set out new plants by profession unless we try to water them diligently and carefully cultivate them to grow. All this must be done with so much effort as the remaining course of religious life of each one depends upon the years immediately after profession."

It is sad, indeed, if the younger religious are entirely neglected and left to themselves after they have had an excellent training from the Novice-master. Then they cannot help forgetting what they have learned in the novitiate, becoming less fervent religious, and gradually straying from the right path and giving themselves over to tepidity. The dangers of perversion are no less after the novitiate than during the novitiate. In fact, the Professed are tempted more than the novices to throw off restraint and self-control, either by bad habits not yet overcome, or by the bad example of others. What is found in the "Methodus Orandi" is confirmed by experience, "It has never been observed that a lax or tepid novice became fervent by profession. Rather on the contrary are novices to be seen fervent and recollected who drop much of their religious discipline and recollection as soon as they are professed."

It is true, novices are not yet perfect when they make profession. Nobody can or does expect this. The year of novitiate is not sufficient to eradicate vices and to implant virtues deeply. Besides, since the novices are usually of younger age, they are unacquainted with many temptations and difficulties which will arrive with increasing years.

Thus the work begun in the novitiate must be followed up and completed, so much the more so as he who has gone up to a higher degree in hierarchical rank, must also be conspicuous for greater sanctity. He who has made simple vows is now bound and obliged to what he did of his own accord in the novitiate. He who is solemnly professed must shine with brighter virtues than when he was simple professed. "The Professed," says Ven. John of S. Samson, "must shun the false liberty of the senses and too great laxity of conscience. For they should realize that after their profession they are obliged more than ever to a complete mortification of their senses and passions and that they cannot fail in this without sin, at least by reason of scandal." And he who aspires to the priesthood or who has already attained it is by that very fact obliged to a greater sanctity, as is written in the Imitation of Christ; "Thou hast not lightened thy burden, but art now bound with a stricter bond of discipline and art obliged to a greater perfection of sanctity."

By the priesthood the bonds of religious profession are not only not loosed but doubled, so that those religious priests think wrongly who excuse their laxity of life by saying that they have ceased being in the number of novices, as though veteran religious did not have to excel the novices in virtue.

Not infrequently religious forgetful of their obligation to strive after perfection try to avoid only mortal sin and do not realize that so they hardly differ from the laity.

The "Methodus Orandi" recounts these causes of religious' easily slipping from their first fervor after profession. "In certain ones a natural disgust itself offers the cause of this remissness, a disgust which covers itself with false excuses in order to escape mortification and to assent to a futile examination of conscience. In others the evil example of those who are already of relaxed discipline is the cause,—an example to which they try out of human respect to conform themselves that they may not displease others or expose themselves to ridicule. In others this remissness is caused by the pernicious teachings and axioms which they hear, entirely contrary to those with which they were imbued in the novitiate."

To these we can add, that in many minds, as we have already said, there lurks a wrong idea of the novitiate. For them the novitiate year is not the beginning of the religious life which is afterward to be unfolded and brought to perfection, but a test, as it were. If this is passed all things will be lawful so that they think to enjoy greater liberty after profession and do not try, since no one compels them, to fulfill their profession "in operis veritate," in the reality of execution. All these evils will be increased, if right after profession the religious are left to their own whim and are not kept away from the other religious. Worse happens if the clerics are scattered through various convents, or are allowed to enter into familiarity with seculars or to take long trips. How can such plants, still tender, be kept from withering?

Nothing, therefore, remains but that all concerned, and in the first place the Master of Professed, seriously watch that the Order may not suffer any harm from such customs.

We do not know which office is more difficult or more important, that of Master of novices or of Professed. Novices indeed are more ignorant in the spiritual life and therefore they must be instructed with greater patience in the elements themselves; but the clerics are usually delighted and somewhat bewitched by their liberty and independence and are more inclined to neglect their exercises of piety on account of thir studies. Since they have contracted obligations by their profession, they think they are entitled to certain rights, especially when they are once ordained, except that they frequently misunderstand their rights and dignity!

Therefore the Prefect of the students or the Spiritual Director must before all things impress on his charges that now those vows to which they have bound themselves must be fulfilled in truth and in deed, and every effort must be made to make greater and greater progress in the way of perfection by true humility and obedience, by renunciation and perfect poverty. The priesthood to which they are certainly aspiring demands this. Now that they have ceased to be held under the close scrutiny of the novitiate, they must of their own accord and responsibility do whatever is prescribed by the Rule, the Constitutions, the Customs and the orders of Superiors, because now they are bound by their vows.

Then he should explain the Rule and Constitutions more deeply than was possible in the novitiate since now because of experience they will understand better.

We are wrong to think that the entire content of Rule and Constitution can be easily and immediately grasped and that no progress can be made in our knowledge; although, for shame! many as novices burning with love and zeal for regularity, seemed to have understood more than afterward when they had become lukewarm. The inner meaning will be evident to the ardent and zealous, whereas it is hidden from the others by reason of their tepidity.

He should also explain the entire doctrine of spiritual life and perfection so that when they are priests, not only they themselves may live holily but they may be able to lead others to holiness also. It will be useful to explain the higher degrees of prayer since these could be touched only cursorily in the novitiate.

Then he should strive to imprint most deeply in the minds of his charges all that has been said about the true spirit of the Order, so that they may become Carmelite priests who are not forgetful of the truly Carmelite life and its chief aim on account of their priesthood or the sacred ministry, but know how to unite prayer and activity.

It is clear that the professed clerics should be imbued with the spirit of the sacred Liturgy so that they may enter more deeply day after day into the treasures of the Divine Office and the sacrifice of the Mass, and that when once ordained, they may celebrate so much more devoutly and with so much more fruit. For this reason the liturgical solemnities should be celebrated with due splendor, since practice is the best instruction.

Candidates are not prepared for so great a ministry in one day or in a brief retreat, but it is a great undertaking to offer to God worthy ministers and faithful dispensers of his mysteries.

The Master will try in vain to accomplish all the foregoing unless he removes whatever cannot be reconciled with the pursuit of perfection. Undoubtedly the pursuit of literature and science may hinder some from persevering in the way of perfection, though this need not be the case. Yes, the study of Philosophy and Theology elevates the mind of youth to God and makes them love God more, if only they are done with a good intention and in due measure. It will be the Master's duty to show those who are applying themselves to their studies how they are not to be drawn away from God, but rather to Him.

Right away he must be on guard that when they go back to their studies they do not begin to despise those things which they have learned in the novitiate. "Some young religious," says the "Methodus Orandi," "are persuaded when they go back to their books, that so far they have learned nothing in the Order, and that now they are going to be taught sublime things. They who think in this way are deprived of light and do not comprehend or esteem the things of God as they ought. For what is taught in the novitiate and in the seminary is the only true and necessary science, inasmuch as the additional knowledge which they have to acquire, is only accessory and accidental and is of less value."

Among the exhortations drawn from the writing of the Venerable Dominic of St. Albert and John of St. Samson, the following are to be found: "Solely and sincerely strive to please God in your new occupation and try to preserve his presence continuously. Not as though you will be able to give your complete attention to study and to God at the same time. This is impossible and it will be necessary to direct your intellect to your study, while in the meantime your will persists in its unvarying intention of loving God and in the desire of pleasing Him. Carefully note that a true lover does not pay attention to the action he is performing to the extent of forgetting his love toward him for whom he is doing the action. Just as an artisan who is making something for his master in the shop, has his mind intent on doing his work right, at the same time strives with his heart and intention, even though without disquiet, to satisfy his master.

"Your application to your studies should be virtuous, i.e., moderated between excessive worry and negligence. Both these extremes are vices. On the one hand you must beware of being neglectful and indifferent to your studies on the plea of not neglecting piety; since God wishes you to attend to them properly, as long as the Order has enjoined them. On the other hand you must likewise beware of excessive solicitude, which is a certain avidity or greediness of mind and which would force you to be carried to your books by a blind instinct without your ever recalling God, or allowing yourself time for self-knowledge, and for recollection even when you are in your cell. This would be greatly opposed to the practice of pure love, and of the intention of fulfilling only God's will without any will of your own. In these strange impulses of your soul you must employ violence on yourself so that you may not only recite the customary Ave Maria, but also that you may kneel down on your priedieu to check this impulse and gradually to control it."

The exercise of God's presence rightly explained will automatically do this.

Other things offer a much more serious danger than the necessary pursuit of studies, and the Superior must do all in his power to avoid them. We have already spoken of ill-timed conversation with seculars and with other religious which is expressly forbidden by the Constitutions.

But there is little use in keeping our young men from conversing with their brethren and with seculars, if we do not also shut out those things which are done among men. For by reading we enjoy the life of the world. How wisely have not the Supreme Pontiffs forbidden daily papers and magazines in seminaries! But it is harmful also to allow indiscreetly those periodicals which treat of Philosophy, Theology and the other sciences and to suffer the students to neglect their own studies and to apply themselves to other studies and to politics under pretense of preparing themselves for the sacred apostolate. In this fashion their minds are not instructed, but distracted.

The use of the radio is dangerous and contrary to the spirit of Carmel especially for clerics, unless it happens only in common recreation and under the constant supervision of the Master. For not even mature men are so strong and constant as to seek knowledge before enjoyment and never to lose time; much less younger men. The Superior who permits the radio without the aforesaid cautions and restrictions can hardly be said to be free from serious responsibility. In such matters we should not ask whether sin lies in them or not, but whether they are in agreement with the spirit of Carmel whose chief portion is to converse with God. For if we only intend to preserve our religious from manifest sin but do not wish or try to inflame them and to lead them to greater and higher things, as is only fit, of what good is the religious state? We sin against the very nature and essence of the religious state, and not venially either.

Not less cruelly do Superiors treat the Professed, if they apply them before their time to external works or burden them with so many and so great duties and labors that they are kept from their own studies and spiritual exercises. He acts contrary to reason who employs those not fully formed in forming others and does not give them time and place to be properly formed and to drink in more deeply the spirit of Carmel. Thus the evils with which we are afflicted are prolonged forever and good and permanent fruits will never be gathered from neglected trees. Oh that all those whom this concerns, would meditate and understand these things! To provide for present necessities in this fashion is to do nothing else but to pay debts by making greater ones.

The Master will take special care of those who have been initiated into the priesthood before completing their course of studies, and who therefore continue by order of our Constitutions to dwell among the students.

A certain Superior writing to his newly-ordained likened the six years immediately following ordination to those stormy and dangerous years in which we develop from boyhood into manhood and in which usually is decided how each one will turn out. For this reason he advised them to watch themselves and to restrain themselves. And the Decree issued by the Sacred Congregation of Religious on December 1, 1931, speaks of the very great dangers which usually occur in the beginning of the priestly life.

Indeed the temptation lays hold on the newly-ordained priests to show their dignity by considering themselves exempt from the laws by which the other students continue to be bound, and for this reason, they try to vindicate to themselves privileges and exemptions, and treat with greater freedom, or shall I say insolence?, with Superiors; seek familiarity and conversation with the other Fathers, withdraw from the society of their fellow-students; seduced by vain glory or false zeal and deceived by inexperience they neglect the Rules laid down by the Constitutions for conduct with seculars; they despise the silence and solitude of the cloister and their cell; they omit their studies and their spiritual exercises and no longer having to fear being withheld from Sacred Orders, begin to lead a more comfortable life.

In fact, the Decree just quoted refers not only to newly-ordained priests who must yet complete their fourth year, but even to those who have completed their studies. "Superiors should watch," says the Decree, "that the young men once ordained and having finished their studies, be not left to themselves, but should have them under their special care for some time. In order that this may be the more easily done, the Superiors will assign these young men to houses where perfect regular observance flourishes, in order that they may go through a special novitiate according to each one's ability. In the meantime they should continue their studies and should show steady progress in them according to the prescription of Canon Law, which orders that religious priests for five years after the completion of their studies should be examined each year by learned and serious Fathers in the various branches of sacred learning opportunely indicated beforehand."

The Prefect of the students, therefore, should keep those who have not yet completed their studies from the company of the rest; he should teach them to think rightly of their priestly dignity so that they may not go astray in the beginning of their priestly career and having hit upon rocks, perish. Not rarely even religious of advanced age seek others to follow them and to agree with their opinions and customs hardly spiritual under the guise of friendship and good will; and so the minds of the younger ones are easily deceived; in fact, they allow themselves to be influenced rather by such men than by their superiors.

Let the Prefect, therefore, not allow his charges to undergo such influence; but let him like a good shepherd defend his sheep against the wolves as much as he can. This can be done the more easily, if all the students occupy a special section of the monastery.

On account of the dangers described, all those concerned are seriously obliged to consider whether there is any real advantage for the candidates or for the Order to have them ordained before time. And certain material gains are not the only consideration! All circumstances should be considered. It does not seem to favor the training of our young men, to ask and to grant dispensations from the laws of the Church or of the Order for every slight reason. Why, may we ask, were such laws made? Superiors should not out of cowardice yield to impetuous and importunate requests, inasmuch as they must give a severe reckoning before God for every ordination.

It will not be amiss to reproduce the admonitions which are given in the "Methodus Orandi" to the junior professed for preserving the spirit of the novitiate.

First comes negative advice.

1. Never to suffer the esteem of their vocation, their love and fervor to grow cold or to be extinguished.

2. Never to be dissipated by external employments and never of their own will to seek any.

3. Not to choose anything of their own will or to desire to do so.

4. To avoid particular friendships.

5. To flee vain curiosity and distractions.

6. Not to be too familiar with older religious.

7. Not to follow the example of those who have already become lax in discipline.

8. Never to approve any speech, pronouncement or dogmatizing contrary to perfection.

9. Never to give way to false and biting zeal or to rash judgments.

Then comes positive advice.

1. What must young religious observe between themselves and God? Cultivate the spirit of devotion; always keep a tender conscience; always have a good intention.

2. What must young religious observe toward their most loving mother, the Order? Always, everywhere and in all things to be a good example to all. Imitate the more fervent. Love the common good. Be dutiful and obedient also to the Brethren.

3. What must young religious observe toward themselves? Before all aim at spiritual progress. Spend time properly and well. Cultivate properly both the interior as well as the exterior man.

Here there are as many subjects for conferences to the students as there are counsels. No one should think such doctrine too high or too mystical; for we are obliged to strive for perfection and we can desire nothing higher than that. And the means must be in proportion to our perfection.

Without doubt a great burden has been placed on the shoulders of the Master or Prefect. He also no less than the Novice-master must be asked not merely to offer advice and instruction to his professed, but also to assure himself that his advice and precepts are being carried out. No detail should be overlooked. This is necessary that our young men really may become accustomed to good discipline and prompt obedience and persevere in it; but especially that the Master himself may know them and more easily direct them so that at the proper time he may be able to propose them or not, in peace of conscience and certain knowledge, for solemn profession or sacred Orders.

It is certain that the watchfulnes of Superiors is sometimes resented by young religious, filled as they are with a desire for liberty and a vain opinion of themselves, inasmuch as they think they have grown up and no longer need a nurse. But let the good Master not be deceived! Blessed is he if he has such good subjects that they always and everywhere do their duty promptly and are mindful of what they are told. Then let him thank God and the Guardian Angels for a burden that has been made so light.

However, one must not take such things easily for granted, especially when the young men entrusted to one for training have been gathered from different countries and from different schools perhaps below standard. Frequently one finds out in a short time how necessary vigilance is and it often happens that those, who complain most about surveillance are weakest and least trustworthy when the surveillance is lifted. Those who are good religious readily grasp that it is the Superior's duty to watch and that he must fulfill it; they do not wonder but wish the Superior to act thus.

Besides, in other Orders great and famous, not only the young, but also the older ones are usually under surveillance. Otherwise what are Superiors for and why do we continue to elect them? We must note what St. Thomas says, "Just as one who owes money must seek out his creditor when the time comes to pay the debt, so he who has the special responsibility for another must seek him to correct him for his fault."

Since the Master of Professed has many difficult duties, "he should be free from all duties and offices which can hinder his care and guidance of the students."

Nothing can be more important than the proper guidance and education of those who will constitute the Order in time to come. To prefer another work to this great work is a crime and the greatest injustice.

CHAPTER III

The Duties of Superiors

1

Major Superiors

IT SHOULD be a matter of deepest concern to the higher superior to bring about an increase in his Province and not merely to preserve it in its present state. He cannot, therefore, be indifferent to the acquiring of new members and to their proper training. If he wishes conscientiously to fulfill the office of father of the family committed to him, he must give them his special attention. Although immediate care of the novices and students devolves upon their respective masters, the higher superior is primarily answerable for them.

That this fruitful increase may take place it is above all things necessary that good discipline obtain throughout the Province. If the Province lacks good religious observance, God will not bless it with increase; He will moreover permit the new candidates He has sent to be estranged from it and leave it in disgust; or if they remain, to be infected with the bad example and perish. For the Order that fails to measure up to the ideal God has of it has lost its right not only to increase but even to exist and is good for nothing but to be cast out and destroyed. It has become a useless branch on the tree of the Church and if the Divine Goodness still suffers it to remain there for a while, it is with a view to the reform of the religious and to their efforts to repair their strength when religious discipline has been reestablished. It is only when the Provincial puts forth every effort to foster the true

Carmelite spirit in his Province that he can with a good conscience petition Divine Providence to send new members.

No one will deny that an adequate number of members is indispensable to the proper carrying out of religious discipline. When the number of members has been greatly reduced and the same number of monasteries retained, the individual religious becomes unequal to the burden of duties that devolves upon him and is unable properly to fulfill them. Love of religious discipline and the desire to promote it should urge the Provincial to be solicitous for an increase in membership.

This solicitude must begin with the Marianate as the Constitutions of our Order point out in Chapter Two. Nor must the Provincial shrink from establishing the Marianate on account of difficulties or expense, for in our age it is hardly possible to bring about growth in the Province in any other way. But the Marianate that is founded according to the requirements of our Constitutions must be of such a character that it is a kind of preparatory seminary of our Order, otherwise both effort and expense will be wasted. First of all a rector should be appointed, endowed with zeal and experience, who will train the candidates in the spirit of the Order. Not everyone is qualified for this office. And who will place the training of those in whom rests his whole future hope, in the hands of the unqualified? Even in the order of nature beds of seedlings require the care of more experienced gardeners than do ordinary gardens.

Nor should be forgotten what is said in art. 23 of the Constitutions, "Higher superiors should make it a point frequently to visit in person the scholasticates of the Province; they should diligently watch over the instructions whether literary, scientific, or religious, that are given to the students; they should fully acquaint themselves with the character, piety, vocation and progress of each student." If the Superiors are negligent in this matter, many unworthy candidates will be the longer supported by the Order, while many who are worthy and fit will not persevere.

Superiors must not receive candidates into the Novitiate before they have finished their classical studies, according to the ruling of the Church. A plant that is not properly cultivated cannot in due time bring forth the expected fruit, nor will the Order gain a good name among the faithful if it is inferior to other Orders in learning. If there is no one in the convents able to teach the required courses, common sense demands that our Mariani be sent to a school that is properly equipped. It is unfair to our candidates not to give them a standard course, so that afterwards they are forced to remain in the Order because through lack of proper training they are unfit to earn a living in the world or are unqualified to enter the ranks of the secular clergy. Vocations secured for the Order by such dubious proceedings do not come from God. They are a liability to the Order, not an asset. The freedom of their profession required by the Law may thus be called in question. Let us cultivate vocations given by God in a way worthy of Divine vocations so that they may in due time bear abundant and permanent fruit for God.

Hugh of St. Francis in his book "The Ideal of a Religious Superior" or "The Life of Venerable Philip Thibault, Reformer of the Carmelites of France," advises the Novice-master to investigate with what industry and ability his novices applied themselves previously to their studies, "since," he says, "it is most difficult for a negligent and deficient student to become a good religious."

The major superior should have special solicitude for the novitiate. He may take Father Dominic of St. Albert as an example who although he looked after all with the greatest care, made special provisions for the proper education of the young members, for he knew well that for the safeguarding, increasing, and strengthening of religious discipline special care must be directed to the novitiate and the houses of studies as to the root of all progress or decline in an Order. He must therefore see to it that the novitiate conforms to the requirements of Canon Law and the regulations of our Constitutions. He must receive only those whom he finds after a careful examination to be worthy candidates for our Order and he must not let himself be enamoured of numbers at the expense of quality. It is more becoming to make a selection of prospective candidates than to urge them to enter. Such a careful selection will not only prevent useless expense and safeguard the Order from many evils, but will render the education of worthy candidates easier. If the major superior does not wish greviously to burden his conscience, let him carefully observe the regulations concerning the reception of novices. It is a bit of prudence to seek the advice of others and not to place too much trust in one's own judgment.

"The master of novices must take what is given to him, and what is given to him is often far from what he would desire!" is the lament of a certain Novice-master. It is unjust to the Novice-master to force him to undertake the training of the untrainable who are proof against all external influence. Such a prospect of profitless burdens and toil is disheartening. One who has had experience can testify how difficult and wearisome it is to deal with those who have no true vocation and who will never become true religious.

The proper training of novices is greatly hindered by a lack of regular discipline in the novitiate-house, so that while the novices are taught one thing by the master, they are taught quite the opposite by the conduct of the members of the community. What an obstacle to the training of novices! With what good reason the Codex demands that "Superiors shall place in the novitiate-house only such religious as are exemplary for religious observance!" Otherwise the Novice-master will find his instructions for the most part falling on deaf ears, or he will need constantly to warn the novices not to act like the older religious. Some of the best novices finding themselves in the dilemma of discrepancy between novitiate teaching and the general practice, may solve the difficulty by choosing the alternative of joining another religious community or returning to the world. Therefore the Superior must of necessity see to it that there is perfect religious observance in the novitiate-house, nor shall he permit it to be disturbed or violated by anyone. This is the best instruction and training of novices, nor is there any easier and at the same time more efficacious way of inspiring them with the true spirit of Carmel. They will find no difficulty in learning to live as becomes Carmelites.

Let the Superior therefore preserve and guard with solicitude those whom God has given him. On the other hand let him not retain those who through lack of necessary virtues and qualifications seem not to be called by God to the Carmelite life.

The Provincial must not confine his solicitude merely to the novices but must extend it also to the clerical students. Moreover, according to what we have said and the Holy See has decreed, he must extend his watchfulness also to the newly ordained priests who have completed their studies.

To satisfy this obligation it is necessary in the first place that he seriously consider the appointment of a prefect of the students who will guide and assist the students during these important years so filled with difficulty and danger. This appointment is of the greatest weight and it is evident that not everyone is qualified. It is wrong to entrust the students to newly ordained priests who themselves should still be under vigilance, and who on account of their youth can hardly wield proper authority, especially if but a short while before they were in the ranks of the same students. Canon Law prescribes an age of thirty years.

The Provincial should take care that the studies are properly performed and he should not admit anyone to Sacred Orders who has not sufficiently applied himself to his studies. He should moreover provide for a strict compliance with the requirements of the decree of the Sacred Congregation of Religious of Dec. 1, 1931, in reference to simple and solemn profession.

If clerics are ordained before the completion of the fourth year of theology the Provincial must not assign them to other work to the neglect or omission of their studies, and this is a grave matter of conscience for him. And he must not think that time is being lost, for those who have completed their courses will be able to do far more work and far better work than those who have been assigned to duties prematurely.

Even after the completion of their studies, according to the decree referred to above, the newly ordained must be placed in houses where there is perfect religious observance, and the Provincial is bound to inform the Sacred Congregation in his five-yearly report concerning the yearly examination of the newly ordained for five years, and to state the reasons for exemptions from these examinations if he has granted any.

The Provincial should be convinced that he promotes the welfare of the Province and the Order better in proportion to the care he bestows upon the young members. He should not expect to reap the fruits of his labors at once, but he should wait patiently even in the face of difficulties and straits and the importunate urging of other religious, until with God's help the fruit has matured.

In this way the Provincial will leave an excellent inheritance to his successors; God will reward him and future generations will bless his memory. If he acts otherwise, he may free himself for the time being from difficulties; but he will leave them, and greater ones, to posterity, unless indeed they overtake him in his own time. The evil done to the Province and Order will be irremediable. The education and training of the young members must of necessity be complete if they are afterwards to educate and train others. More than once the Fathers at the Convention lamented the fact that often those are appointed to the office of master or prefect who were themselves never properly instructed and hence do not know how to teach and train others.

The superior must not forget the rest of the religious on account of the young members, but on account of the young members he should make every effort to have the rest faithfully observe the Rule and Constitutions and live religiously, so that through contact with them the young religious will be more easily and more effectively trained. To this end it is important that the Provincial hold the prescribed visitations regularly and thoroughly; he must see to it that the regulations he makes at them are carried out; and he should assist and strenuously defend the local Superior in the enforcing of discipline and the Master in the training of the young religious, against any religious who may oppose them. With united forces progress is assured even though all cannot be accomplished in one stroke. And if there are opponents and the Superior meets with contradictions, let him weigh the opinions of his adversaries and follow what is good in them; at the same time he should not forget that Our Lord too was the victim of unjust judgment and obloquy. It is sufficient if he strives with a good conscience to fulfill his office.

2

Local Superiors

It is the duty of the local Superior diligently to care for the flock committed to him both in spiritual and in temporal matters as having to render an account of both on the Last Day to the Just Judge and Great Pastor. "The Prior shall above all things see to it that religious discipline is diligently observed."

Let him keep in mind what has been said about the spirit of Carmel, put it into practice himself and require his community to do the same.

In particular Priors who have in their convents Mariani or novices or professed students, should for reasons given above, diligently carry out the following: Let them not permit the work of the Masters to be hindered or destroyed by the other religious, or let the rest of the religious have any communication with the novices or students. In vain does the Master forbid the novices or students to converse or associate with the priests or lay brothers, unless the Prior takes measures to prevent solicitation to this on the part of the Priests and lay brothers.

The Prior should work hand in hand with the Masters and he should not burden them with work foreign to their office. He must never belittle their authority or himself grant to the novices or students (except for truly grave reasons) what their Masters have refused. Nothing hinders training so effectually as discord among Superiors which the young shrewdly know how to turn to their advantage. If any differences arise these should be settled peaceably in secret, or referred to the Provincial.

It is, however, the Prior's duty to see that the Masters and Prefects properly fulfill their office.

The Prior must give attention also to the lay brothers and not leave them to their own resources. If lay brothers do not receive the instructions that the Common Law and our Constitutions prescribe, it is no wonder if they are out of harmony with their state. They cannot be content and ready to labor and make sacrifices if spiritual bread is never offered to them, and they are left more destitute in this than seculars who freely request this bread and perhaps find it abundantly at our doors. Let not our own be fed with the crumbs that fall from the tables of others!

According to the ruling of the Constitutions and of the Rule itself the Prior should hold a Chapter of Faults every week. In it he should not merely condemn indiscriminately certain faults, but he should offer an orderly exposition of the doctrine of religious perfection, and with due preparation an explanation of the Rule and Constitutions, so that his community may be more and more animated with the spirit of Carmel.

If he should notice any one committing a fault he should admonish him, and if the case calls for it he should not be afraid to inflict punishment for the amendment of the delinquent, lest through the silence or neglect of the shepherd, the sheep perish and gradually the entire flock be infected. Many scandals would never have happened if Superiors had in due time raised their voices and had not through human respect or timidity or sheer neglect kept silence. "For Superiors," say the Constitutions, "are bound to correct the faults of their subjects and to put forth every effort to lead them to amendment; for which reason they should in due time charitably offer fatherly admonitions and exhortations. But if these are ineffective they should inflict salutary penances and proportionate punishments." And "We wish and ordain that violators of the Constitutions be severely punished, particularly Superiors who are negligent in observing them or in punishing delinquents." It was said to all Superiors: "Preach the word; be instant in season and out of season reprove, entreat, rebuke in all patience and doctrine."

Finally he should teach as well by deed and example as by word, and in watchfulness ascertain that all are living and acting as becomes religious, lest while the Father of the household is asleep the enemy sow the cockle. "Blessed is that servant whom the Lord when he cometh and knocketh on the door shall find watching."

CHAPTER IV

The Obligations of All Religious in General

ALL THE rest of the religious should work together with zeal and true love of the Order for the internal and external growth of the Order. It is for them to merit the blessing of God by their religious lives and through their good example to inspire the young members with a love for the Order to teach them the true Carmelite spirit. How many religious vocations are lost through the bad example and scandals of the religious themselves! Youths because of their inexperience of human nature and because of their desire of a perfect life expect all religious to be perfect, and not yet having learned to distinguish between persons and things, they are easily deceived and lose their vocation. Woe to the world because of scandals, says the Lord. But while it is necessary that there should be scandals in the world it is not necessary in religion. All the greater is the sin of those through whom scandal comes into religion.

Therefore all should seriously strive to live the truly Carmelite life both because of their own salvation and because of the vocations of others, and let them fulfill in very deed what they have vowed. All should diligently study the Rule and Constitutions, lest while they desired to be Carmelites and imagined they were, in the end they find they are far from the spirit of Carmel. He who disregards one law is made a transgressor of the whole law. Not merely one or the other article is to be observed but the whole Carmelite Law. And let no one form a lax conscience in this matter on the ground that he bound himself of his own accord to strive after perfection. Not without reason do our Constitutions give the following admonition: "That our Brethren may in very deed faithfully comply with obedience let them diligently study those things that are obligatory under obedience, as are the following: The Rule, the Constitutions, the Ceremonial, the Ritual, and the other liturgical books according to our rite, the instructions and commands of Superiors; and let each one according to its obligation observe them. And therefore let each one diligently read these Constitutions." By way of comment on the words, "according to its obligation,"—although the Constitutions do not bind under sin but only to the undergoing of punishment, many of the prescriptions of the Constitutions are nothing else than an explanation of the Rule and therefore bind under venial sin because of the Rule, as is to be said particularly in regard to the observance of silence and the fasts.

You were not bound to take the vows, but you are bound to keep them.

Let us not forget the doctrine of fraternal correction. While there are many murmurers and detractors, there are few that have the courage to lead the erring brother into better ways. Much is lacking in a religious house where fraternal correction is never given, or is never received with humility and gratitude. We considered the example of S. Mary Magdalene above. "When any sister absented herself from the community she herself approached her to give her friendly admonition or referred the matter to the Superior that the defect might be corrected."

All should petition God for vocations; both clerical and lay, for our Order and if the occasion offers, try to bring worthy candidates into the Order. To this end all should always conduct themselves as true religious before seculars, and should be mindful of art. 18 of the Constitutions: "Just as the internal perfection of our Order consists in fervent charity, so its external honor and beauty consists in becoming and modest intercourse with seculars"; and art. 188, which says: "Both within and without the convent all should control their senses, particularly the eyes, the ears and the tongue, keep themselves in true humility and manifest it for the edification of others in their words, their modest countenance and grave bearing." Likewise art. 183 should not be forgotten: "No one should dare to have such relationship with seculars that through their excessive familiarity the secrets of the convent may be revealed."

The good will of seculars can be gained for the Order by apostolic works rightly undertaken and performed and through the publication of books and periodicals. When the Order has thus become better known we will gain more vocations.

Let us learn a lesson from S. Mary Magdalene of Pazzi. She always held religious life and the religious state in the highest esteem; she was accustomed to call it the pupil of the eye of God, the delight of heaven, an earthly paradise, a heavenly land. She exhorted all to love the religious state as a mother. And this is done, she says, when there is obedience and the observance of the Rule and Constitutions, even though the things in them seem trifles, for they are ordained of the Holy Spirit. She was not only most observant herself but also most zealous that the others should be so likewise. That she might be assured that strict observance would continue in her monastery, she induced many to promise that they would remain firm in maintaining discipline. For she said that those who understood the perfection of the religious state should at their death leave as an inheritance to posterity their religious observance that it may be perpetuated.

There may be some who when they think of the crises,through which the Order has passed and the fearful injury it has suffered from them, will be tempted to grow faint-hearted and lose hope of the Order's ever returning to its former splendor. But since Our Blessed Mother has promised to S. Peter-Thomas that the Order will endure to the end of time, let us do what our state requires of us and not fear for the future. With our forces united, our hope established in God and the Blessed Virgin Mary of Mt. Carmel, and our souls penetrated with the spirit of sacrifice, let us beseech God that we may not be a hindrance to the realization of our Blessed Lady's promise!

APPENDIX

Instructing Novices to Pray

REV. JOHN HAFFERT, *O. CARM.*

SINCE the true Carmelite must be pre-eminently a man of prayer one of the principal duties of the Novice-master is to teach his novices to pray. Time and time again must he instruct them in "the methods of meditating," as our Constitutions say (Art. 326), "and in the various ways of praying and of directing their actions to God with the practice of the Presence of God, so that they may become lovers of the interior life." To become lovers of the interior life means to become lovers of prayer, for the interior life is a life of constant communion with God. If we succeed in making our novices lovers of prayer we have established in them a principle that will make them and keep them truly spiritual men. A love for prayer soon gives birth to the habit of prayer, and to be in the state of prayer is an essential part of the Carmelite life. To make them lovers of prayer, how can it be done?

Is it not true that even after repeated instructions on the true nature of mental prayer, novices and also older religious, confound the form of prayer with its nature and in consequence devote most of their time and energy to the preliminaries or mechanics of prayer without arriving at the reality itself. The result is that after a while they begin to tire of meditation as a fruitless and difficult task and are pleased with every opportunity to shirk its performance. The novice-master must therefore again and agin instruct the novices that true prayer is, as St. Theresa says, a conversation with God, the loving conversation of the child of God with his Heavenly Father. The principal object of mental prayer is God, the living God, our Lord Jesus Christ, His Person, His teaching, His words, His example. Two persons are engaged in it, the soul and God—the soul sometimes speaking to God and more often remaining like Mary at His feet in silent, loving attention to the precious words that may fall from His lips. The principal object of meditation is not the exercise of the intellect on some abstract truth even though the purpose may be to move the will to good resolutions, nor is it the examination of self nor the search for self-knowledge. All this does not constitute prayer. If we compare meditation to the reflections that the business map makes to improve his business we are giving a comparison that does not illustrate that meditation which is a prayer; it is an illustration only of the preparation or preliminary exercise of the meditation and may rather give the novice wrong ideas on the nature of meditation than enlighten him. So long as the soul is engaged only with its own reflections it is not praying. There is no doubt that such reflections are necessary—nil volitum nisi praecognitum; they enlighten the intellect and render it pliant; they are the material that the intellect gathers to enkindle the heart. Particularly in the beginning of the spiritual life they are indispensable—but prayer begins only when the heart set on fire turns to God and lovingly communicates with Him. For prayer is a matter of the heart. It is written of Mary that she kept the words of Jesus in her heart. Sapiens cor suum tradidit ad vigilandum diluculo ad Dominum qui fecit ilium et in conspectu Altissimi deprecabitur.

Let the novice then understand that meditation is a heart to heart talk with God, the heart of a child trustfully, lovingly unveiling itself to its Heavenly Father; that it is the heart of a child telling its love to the heart of Jesus, and listening to Jesus telling of His great love for His child. Let him realize that it is of the essence of prayer to be an intercourse with the living Person of Jesus Christ and through Him and with Him, with the Father and the Holy Ghost, a heart to heart talk with God who knows and loves and listens and responds. What a sanctifying, uplifting, spiritualizing effect such communication with God must have! Even if the meditation resulted in no explicit resolutions, the soul would be sanctified by this very association with God and made more Godlike by it. It can easily be seen that the effect of such prayer cannot confine itself merely to the hour of prayer but will extend itself throughout the day and place its character upon all the actions of the day. It will sustain the soul in trials, strengthen it in temptations, inspire it in its activities. It will little by little estrange the heart from the things of earth and fix it on the things of Heaven, or rather it will clear the vision of the soul to see at all times the great, all-loving God in His creatures. Such is the aim or purpose of meditation, to Place the soul in the state of prayer, in the state of continual intercourse with God. "You must pray always and not faint," says our Lord, and St. Paul: "Pray without ceasing!" "I will praise the Lord at all time; His praise is always in my mouth."

Novices must be made to understand that the aim of prayer is union with God. If their meditation is well made it will sanctify their whole day. No matter how much work they may have to do or how many duties they may have to perform, their meditation will envelop all in an atmosphere of prayer, and daily shed new light upon their souls and enkindle new fires of love in their hearts. Such is the life of the true Carmelite and the soul of that life is formed in the exercise of such true prayer.

What guidance shall be given to the novice to make his meditation true prayer? There is very definite and persevering effort required on the part of the novice. While prayer is the work of the Holy Spirit within him his own cooperation is necessary, and his meditations will be fruitful only in proportion to the earnestness and fidelity with which he prepares himself for them and performs them. The Novice-master must teach him the various methods of meditation but the ultimate choice of a particular method must be left to the novice himself, for a method that may be a help to one may be a hindrance to another. Whatever method the novice may choose, the Novice-master would do well to insist on the following practices.

Several hours before the exercise of meditation takes place the novice should prepare the matter of his meditation and determine the fruit to be derived from it. This preparation can be made at night before retiring for the morning meditation and some time during the day for the evening meditation. It consists in familiarizing himself with the subject-matter of the meditation and dividing it into points. This preparation is a very great help to the novice and does much towards disposing him for communion with God during the meditation. It would be well worth while putting this preparation into the regular schedule of the day and determining a definite time for its performance.

When in the beginning of the meditation the novice places himself in the presence of God, he must strive to realize that he is in the presence of his own dear Heavenly Father, of his Divine Brother, of the Sweet Guest of his soul; that this God who is within his very being loves him personally, individually as if no other human being existed; that the powerful, deep, burning love of his Heavenly Father is beaming upon him, His child. O my God, Thou who knowest me by my name and Who art thinking of me, Thou lovest me! This realization of the personal love of God for the soul is the foundation of devotion, the soul of prayer. Such realization of the presence of God warms the heart and from the very beginning of the meditation places the soul into an attitude of prayer. It gives rise to acts of love, of humility, of sorrow for sin, and of confident petition for help. It gives rise to generous impulses, to oblation of self, and binds the soul most intimately to God. In such realization of the presence of God lies the secret of a good meditation. If this first act of the meditation, the placing of oneself in the presence of God, is not done well it may leave the whole exercise cold and fruitless. How important it is that the novice begin his meditation well, and from the very beginning place himself into an atmosphere of prayer. Now the mere recalling of the truth of the omnipresence of the Majesty of God is not sufficient for this; it must be a realization of the presence of a Divine Person, or of the three Divine Persons, who love him with an unspeakable, personal, undivided love. This realization of the personal love of God for him will make him feel that he is alone with God. "When thou shalt pray, enter into thy chamber and having shut the door, pray to thy Father in secret." He will enter into the Heart of Jesus and expose his own heart to burning fires of that great Heart, and his Father who seeth in secret will repay him.

When the novice begins his reflection on the subject-matter of his meditation he will do it in the presence of his own, all-loving God. Jesus will speak to him, for has He not solemnly promised to do so? I will ask the Father and He will give you another Paraclete. He will teach you all truth and bring to your minds all the things that I have said to you. Thus from the very beginning to the end of the meditation there is contact between the soul and God; there is loving communion and the eliciting of many acts of the affections—thanksgiving, oblation, petition.

I think the foregoing suggestions, if carried out, will help to develop the spirit of prayer in our young men. Without that spirit, no matter how much learning they may have, they will not be fit instruments in the hands of God. Mount Carmel is synonomous with prayer, and Carmelite, with Man of Prayer. How grave is the obligation of the Novice-master to develop in his novices the spirit of prayer! He must be untiring in his efforts to instruct them properly and adequately in the excellence, benefits, and importance of prayer; in the various methods and ways of prayer. If he finds that some take no interest in the subject and show a dislike for prayer, he should by all means counsel their dismissal;—they are not fit for the Carmelite life.

Not only should the Novice-master be untiring in his instructions on prayer, but he should also diligently watch over the carrying out of his instructions. He should question each novice from time to time on the subject of prayer and inquire how he is carrying out the instructions he has received; how he prepares his meditations; what method he is using; whether his meditations are really a prayer as described above; whether his meditations are influencing his conduct during the day and bringing him more and more to raise his heart to God during the day in aspirations and good intentions. If the novice is experiencing difficulties, he will inquire into the cause and see whether the difficulty arises from a lack of sufficient effort on the part of the novice; whether it arises from a spirit of worldliness still clinging to him; whether he needs a change of subject or of method, etc. Such investigations the Novice-master should frequently hold, calling each novice to him privately. Let him also pray fervently that God may bless his novices with the abundance of His Gifts of prayer, of piety and devotion.

The Liturgical Training of the Novices

REV. ANGELINUS KOENDERS, *O. Carm.*

SACRED liturgy, considered juridically, is the ecclesiastical regulation of public worship. Objectively, however, it is the sum total of symbols, texts, and actions established by the Church to express and make known her worship of God. "By the Church," I say; i.e., by that perfect society, by that mystical body of which every baptized man, lay and cleric, is a member. From this it follows that whenever the priest performs a liturgical act, he does not act in his own name, but in the name either of Christ or of the Church, i.e., in the name of all who belong to the Church.

A knowledge of liturgy, and therefore training in liturgy is useful, in fact, necessary for all. Every man has four obligations to God, namely, that he adore, supplicate, thank, and propitiate God. But he cannot acquit himself of these obligations in a better way than by the acts which comprise the liturgy. Although the layman employs the ministry of the priest in practicing his religion, he must have some understanding of those acts which are called liturgical. Therefore, he may not remain entirely ignorant of the liturgy. Wherefore, also, the movement now being furthered in the Western Church,—thanks to the stimulation by Pius X, who wished to restore all things in Christ,—namely, to have the laity instructed in liturgical matters, is the source of much satisfaction. Nor is this without abundant fruit both exteriorly, by the solemnity and care with which the liturgy is celebrated, as well as interiorly, by the ready knowledge, good will and increase of spiritual life in all.

A fortiori, liturgical knowledge is necessary for every priest, not merely for his own spiritual profit, but because liturgy is, to speak truly, a clerical science.

For the cleric, and especially the priest, holds first place in the liturgy. It is he who acts in the place of Christ our Saviour in the oblation of the Immaculate Lamb. It is he who offers praise to God in the name of the Church and who carries the gifts and sacrifices before the divine Majesty in the name of all the faithful, his brethren, to whom he returns to pour over them the divine benefits.

In order that the priest may better discharge his duty of mediator, he ought to penetrate more deeply into the meaning and historical progress of those actions in which, after Christ, he is the chief actor. He will never better understand the sanctity and the sublimity of the sacrifice of the Mass and what pertains to it than when he attentively learns how Holy Mother Church in the course of ages has practiced and most solemnly celebrated this most august "Actio." He will never better and more fruitfully recite his Office than when he tries his best to know the essence of his Breviary, the meaning of the

Psalms, the evolution of the liturgical year with its various seasons and feasts. And although the Sacraments and Sacramentals do not primarily belong to the liturgy since they have not been instituted to praise God, but to sanctify souls, still the ceremonies and prayers, which together constitute the rite of administration have been ordained by the Church; and the priest who has been appointed the minister of Christ and dispenser of His mysteries, will so much more carefully and attentively carry them out as he himself has caught their meaning by a study of liturgy.

Besides this advantage for his priestly life, the cleric can gain another from the study of sacred liturgy—assistance, namely, in the other branches of clerical studies; for example, Dogmatic Theology. All liturgical actions, especially those that occur on feasts and at the seasons of the Ecclesiastical year are most vivid representations of the truths of our Faith and can, therefore, be better grasped and understood by means of the liturgy than can ordinarily be done by purely scholastic arguments. How clearly is the dogma of Our Lord's Incarnation illustrated in the formularies of the three Christmas masses, as well as in the psalms, responsories, writings of the Fathers as found in the office of the day! Dogmatic Theology can give arguments for the redemption of the human race, but this redemption will be more thoroughly understood and realized through that which the Missal and the Breviary place before our eyes in Lent and Passion-tide.

Moreover, everyone can see that the study of Canon Law is helped by Sacred Liturgy because these two sciences frequently meet. Likewise, Church History will be better understood and will be undertaken with greater pleasure if the study of the sacred rites which are so closely connected with Church History and seem to vitalize it, is actually associated with this science of things long past and in one sense dead.

However, we shall have to treat at greater length of the third reason why we consider liturgical training necessary. This reason is of greatest importance not only in general, but especially with reference to our thesis which has our novices in view. It can be stated thus: The study of sacred liturgy is very fruitful in the spiritual life of all; therefore, liturgical training is a very desirable, yes, a necessary part of ecclesiastical training, and therefore, also, of the training of our novices.

The purpose of the novitiate year, as our Constitutions say, is to form the soul of the novice by means of pious meditations, assiduous prayer, in learning those things which pertain to the vows and the virtues, in exercises fitted to root out effectually the roots of vices, to restrain the emotions of the soul and to acquire virtues. All this can be summarized in these words, "The end of the novitiate is to give the first direction to the spiritual life of the novices so that after they have made their profession they may tend to religious perfection." From which it follows that during the novitiate the spiritual life of our novices must be developed by the means enumerated by our Constitutions.

These means with good reason also demand liturgical training. It cannot be denied that there is a mutual reaction between the liturgy and our spiritual life.

The liturgy considered as the sum total of the various acts of religion, springs from the natural desire and necessity of our heart to express in a material way our faith and love in God and our dependence on Him. The more firmly man's soul is convinced of its entire dependence on God, the better will it perform its duties towards God, even exteriorly. If, however, a man has liturgical training, he will more lovingly and carefully do those things which are prescribed by the liturgy, and in this way he will learn to live the life which is called liturgical. In proportion as this liturgical life becomes perfect, man will understand his dependence upon God and so there will rise up in him the desire of joining himself to God. Thus, the liturgy nourishes our soul for a firmer belief, a stronger love, and a more faithful service of God; the spiritual life profits by the liturgy since the liturgy nourishes our supernatural life. Thus is verified what we often ask: "Da nobis proficiendo celebrare et celebrando proficere." "Grant that as we progress we may celebrate, and as we celebrate we may progress." The Sacred Liturgy employs various means to nourish and increase this our spiritual life:

(1) Exhortation. Both in celebrating the sacrifice of the Mass as well as in performing the Divine Office the sacred liturgy draws many parts from Sacred Scripture and the writings of the Fathers. Such are the Epistles and Gospels of Mass, the Psalms and Lessons of the Breviary in which we are exhorted to seek first the kingdom of God, i.e., to live to God and to die to the world and our concupiscences. As though fearing that not all the exhortations contained in these longer readings will bring the desired fruit, it repeats them in shorter form; namely, in the Graduals, Chapters, verses antiphons and other minor parts of Mass and Office.

Therefore, when the novice uses the missal, either in Latin or the vernacular, or when the cleric devoutly recites the Divine Office in choir, at almost every hour there are recalled to his memory his obligations to the divine Majesty; and by reciting his Office, his spiritual life grows from day to day.

(2) Action. It is not possible that piety of soul should not be stirred up by the variety, solemnity and symbolism of the liturgy. Because everything

that is done visibly elevates the mind to the supernatural, makes it tend toward the divine, either by love, gratitude or sorrow,—"ita ut dum per liturgiam visibiliter Deum cognoscimus, per earn in invisibilium amorem rapiamur." "As we learn to know God in a visible way by means of the liturgy, we may by the same liturgy be transported to the love of the invisible." Every truly devout Christian mind is moved by the solemnities of Palm Sunday, Holy Week, Corpus Christi, so that even if it does pay attention to reading or singing the texts, it is refreshed merely by what the eye sees.

(3) Prayer. Since the life of the soul does not grow except with the help of God's grace, the sacred liturgy helps us to implore this grace in the right way. Examine the orations contained in the missal and you will find petitions for obtaining every gift—for temporal and eternal goods, for spiritual and corporal, in harmony with the feast, for present and future needs of body and soul, for the whole Church and for individual members.

The liturgy makes supplication for the soul: "Da nobis fidei, spei et caritatis augmentum." "Ut percipientes hoc munere veniam peccatorum, deinceps peccata vitemus." "Sic transeamus per bona temporalia, ut non amittamus aeterna."

It also makes supplication for the body, knowing that what we receive in the temporal order, according to God's Will is nothing else than a means of closer union with Him, the fount of all good. Only read the supplications for the time of war, for peace, for travelers, for the sick, to ask for rain, to ask for clear weather, for the time of famine and of earthquake.

With what sincerity does not the soul, under the leadership of the liturgy beg pardon. "Miserere mei, Deus—Averte faciem tuam a peccatis meis—Ab occultis meis munda me, Domine." Does our soul stand in need of light and strength in our sad pilgrimage? Listen to her sighs, "Emitte lucem tuam et veritatem tuam—Tu es Deus, fortitudo mea.—Deus refugium meum et virtus."

In every necessity the soul will find in the Sacred Liturgy what to ask and how to ask it, and this for no other reason than "ut spiritum adoptionis (nempe vitam spiritualem) quo filii Dei nominamur et sumus, fideliter custodiamus."

(4) Union. The supernatural life, which is a true life, consists entirely in this as the Saviour Himself said: "That they may know thee, the only true God, and Jesus Christ whom thou hast sent." From this pronouncement it follows that the more perfectly we know God and thence the more powerfully we love Him, either in Himself or through the mediator, Jesus Christ, so much more is this true life perfected in us; for the supernatural life aims at nothing else than that we learn to know and love God as He is. For our spiritual life is strengthened by those very means by which our knowledge and our love are increased. Among these means the Sacred Liturgy does not hold last place. For is not the liturgical year a representation of the Saviour's life whose deeds, wrought for us and for our salvation, are commemorated in a visible and even, if we may say so, a palpable manner; or rather whose virtues, conspicuous throughout His life, are proposed for our enjoyment?

To give a fine example! Examine the Breviary both on the Vigil and Feast of Christmas; read the Responsories of Holy Week; meditate on all that is done in Holy Week and you cannot help seeing clearly and distinctly that the liturgy introduces us into the Heart of Our Redeemer and Head, so that we may taste more and more how sweet is the Lord. Thus it happens that whatever mystery we may celebrate, we shall always obtain that special grace which the Saviour has attached to it and which he has merited for our spiritual life. Every season of the Ecclesiastical Year as well as every liturgical act aims only to make us know and love Christ, and through Him God the Father, better. All this is the same as saying that our spiritual life is strengthened and augmented by the sacred liturgy.

A few words more must be said about a special feature of the supernatural life to which frequently no attention is given in the direction of souls; which consequently is not sufficiently developed and without which the care of the spiritual life in the proper sense remains imperfect. This feature is the social or apostolic life.

We receive our supernatural life not merely for ourselves, but also for all others possessing this spiritual life. "For we, being many, are one bread, one body, all that partake of one bread." (I Cor. X, 17.) "And the eye cannot say to the hand: 'I need not thy help'; nor again the head to the feet: 'I have no need of you' ... And if one member suffer anything, all the members suffer with it; or if one member glory all the members rejoice with it. Now, you are the body of Christ, and members of member." (I Cor. XII, 21-27.)

From this principle it follows that in our spiritual life all things are common to us—health and sickness, joy and sorrow, growth and loss. In other words, the spiritual life excludes all egoism. It makes the soul expand its wings and consider the interests of others as its own. Therefore, he who prays and works merely for himself and follows this one aim, "That I may be a saint; that I may obtain the kingdom of Heaven!" and on this account is more or less indifferent to the interests of others, as for instance, the Church, the Pope, sinners, the missions, etc., lacks in his spiritual life every social and apostolic characteristic. His life is imperfect because it does not sympathize or rejoice with the other members of Christ's mystic body and can be branded with that mark of disgrace, "Am I my brother's keeper?" (Gen. IV. 9.)

But what has the liturgy to do with this? It withdraws us from our narrow egoistic circle and at every moment recalls to our mind that we are members of that body of which Christ is the Head. The heart of him who lives according to the liturgy is enlarged by the thought that our brethren scattered throughout the world in their approach to God, feel as we feel, will as we will. The liturgy demonstrates that the souls of all are connected with the golden thread of supernatural life and love from which arises the sublime communion of Saints. Those who do not know us, pray, offer and satisfy for us and with us, just as we do for and with them, because all things done in the liturgy are done by the whole body for the whole body. For the plural form which is always, or nearly always, employed by the Church clearly shows that the Church is a family whose members pray with and for one another whether they are lay, religious, or clerics. In this respect, the liturgical life is nothing else than a common effort to implant ourselves and strengthen ourselves in Christ so that our whole spiritual life may be molded more and more after the Perfect image of the Son of God. "Until we all meet into the unity of faith, and of the knowledge of the Son of God, unto a perfect man, unto the measure of the age of the fullness of Christ." (Eph. IV, 13.)

Since the end of the novitiate is to assist our candidates in entering the way of Christian perfection, and since on the other hand the Sacred Liturgy is not without reason called, and in fact is the fountain of a more abundant spiritual life, no one can deny that liturgical training can with every right vindicate a place among the various instructions that should be given during the novitiate year.

What, then, is to be understood by the liturgical training of novices?

This training or instruction can be understood in three ways:

(1) Technically, i.e., when the rubrics according to which some liturgical action is to be performed, are learned without reference to the history of this rubric, or to its evolution or meaning. In this respect, liturgical training is necessary for clerical novices so that they may rightly accomplish their duties on the altar and in choir; and for all the novices, including the Brothers, to serve Mass. It is, therefore, a merely material study; which, however, can be vivified by various ascetical motives, as reverence during prayer, the Majesty of God, the praise of God through the Church Triumphant, Communion with holy souls in the Church Militant, and a thousand and one others.

(2) Historically, i.e., the origin and development of the various liturgical actions are investigated at great pains, by examining history and primitive sources. It is not necessary to point out why such a study would be an obstacle rather than an advantage to the aim of the spiritual training of the novices.

(3) Ascetically and historically. This is liturgical instruction properly so called. It embraces an explanation how a liturgical act is to be performed; what is its history; how it has developed; why it has been introduced; what this or that rite means; how in this or the other action some dogma becomes clear; what beautiful connection there is between rites and words; how far ancient usages are still seen in modern practice, etc.

From this explanation it is evident that there are two primary elements, if one may say so, the historical element and the ascetical element. For the novices, however, only the ascetical element should be chosen, because the liturgy should principally be the source of their spiritual life. They should be taught, therefore, the beauty and connection of the feasts and seasons of the Ecclesiastical Year, the meaning of the Divine Office, the supereminence of the supreme liturgical act, the Sacrifice of the Mass, and a method of uniting themselves by means of the missal with the priest in offering this sacrifice according to the mind of the Church and of participating in this sacrifice through Holy Communion. Occasionally, however, recourse must be had to the historical element without which the ascetical explanation would be imperfect and insufficient. If, for instance, the solemnities of Holy Saturday are to be explained, it will be necessary for one who wishes to bring the full beauty of this day to his hearers, to go back to the early ages of the Church and show how in those days Baptism was joined to the celebration of the Lord's Resurrection.

Three dangers, however, should be avoided:

(1) In the liturgical training of the novices the historical features should not hold chief place. Otherwise, it will not be a spiritual training to nourish the interior life, but rather a scientific training to satisfy the desire for knowledge which would better be kept for the Theology course.

(2) The ascetical element should not be treated superficially, i.e., the liturgical point should not be explained without giving solid reasons. Neither is it necessary after the example of medieval writers to explain every detail of a liturgical act and give it an ascetical meaning. Still one must be careful not to neglect every historical reason, especially when originally there was no ascetical meaning.

(3) Out of excessive love of the liturgy, non-liturgical devotions must not be despised. Holy

Mother Church has approved them and they are very advantageous to the spiritual life. Just as it would be unreasonable to overestimate such devotions, so also is it reprehensible to suppress them entirely as though the Sacred Liturgy were the only true devotion. Christ has said: "These things you ought to have done, and not to leave those undone." (Matt. XXIII, 23, 23.) The devotion of the novices to the Sacred Liturgy should indeed be great, but not exclusive.

The liturgical training of our novices should be given not to satisfy their eagerness for study, not even to lay the foundation for their theological studies, but rather to nourish and to expand their spiritual life, that since they form a noble section of the faithful and are aspiring to the priesthood, they may learn to relish and understand the liturgy of the Church. Let them learn, writes Our Holy Father, Pius X of blessed memory, "to return to the primary and necessary source of the Christian spirit, that they may imbibe thence the true Christian spirit by participating actively in the most holy Mysteries and in the public and solemn prayer of the Church."

Our novices by means of the Sacred Liturgy should become more and more interior men, as the Church prays, "ut sacrosancta Mysteria, gratiae tuae operante virtute, et praesentis vitae nos conversatione sanctificent, et ad gaudia sempiterna perducant." Thus will be attained the end which the Church wishes to be attained by the liturgy, "that Christ may be formed in them," and "that in all things God may be honored through Jesus Christ." (I Pet. IV. 11.)

Books Which the Novice-Master Can Consult in Instructing Carmelite Novices

The Carmelite Rule:

1. The brief expositions of the rule written in the 14th century by John Baconthorp and by Siberto de Beka. Consult *De Scriptoribus Scholasticns Saeculi XIV ex Ordine Carmelitarum* of Bartholomeus Maria Xiberta, O. Carm., Louvain 1931.

2. *Expositio Paraenetica in Regulam Carmelitarum*, of B. John Soreth, edited by Daniel a Virgine Maria in *Speculum Carmelitanum*, Antwerp, 1680.

3. *Della Disciplina Regolare* of Hieronymus Gratianus, Venice, 1600.

4. *Opera Omnia* of Ven. Thomas a Jesus, C. D.

5. *Heroica Carmeli Regula* of Valentinus a S. Amando, Cologne, 1682.

6. *Commentarius in Mare Magnum et Regulam Carmelitarum* of John Baptist Lezana, Lyons, 1656.

7. *Disciplina Regliosa en Consideraciones Espirituales y Reflexiones Morales*, of John A. S. Angelo, 1917.

8. *Frutti del Carmelo* of Emmanuel a Jesu Maria, C. D., Naples, 1705.

9. *Il Novizio Carmelitano Instruito dal suo Maestro nello Stato Religioso, Regola e Constituzioni del suo Ordine*, of Ignatius Maria Rossi, Naples, 1764.

10. *Il Giovane dell'Ordine della S. Virgine Maria del Carmine dell'Antica Osservanza Instruito nella sua Regola, ne'suoi Obblighi e ne suoi Privilegi* of Joseph Maria Sardi, Venice, 1737.

11. *Manuale Juris Communis Regularium et Specialis Carmelitarum Discalceatorum, ad Norman Juris Canonici et Nostrarum Constitutionum Accommodatam a P. Nicolao a P. C. M. Ejusdem Ordinis* of Angelus a SS. Corde Jesu, C. D., Burgis, 1929.

12. *Directoire des Petits Offices* of Marcus a Nativitate Virginis, Andegavi, 1679.

13. The various editions of the Carmelite Constitutions edited by John de Alerio in 1324; by Peter Raymund in 1357; by John Baptist Caffardi in 1586; by Pius M. Mayer in 1904, and by Elias Magennis in 1930.

The Compendium of the Constitutions for the Provincials in Italy of John Baptist Rubeo, 1568.

The Constitutions and Decrees edited by the General Chapter in 1593; those of the Congregation of Mantua, Bologna, 1602; and those of the Strictoris Observantiae pro Reformatis of 1637 and 1656.

Lives:

1. St. Magdalene de Pazzi, in *Acta Sanctorum*, on May 25.

2. Venerable Angelus Pauli, in *Analecta Ord. Carm.*, Vol. I.

3. Venerable Michael a Fonte, in *Analecta Ord. Carm.*, Vol. VI.

4. Venerable Philip Theobald, in *Analecta Ord. Carm.*, Vol. VII.

5. *La Vie du Venerable Pere Philippe Thibaut*, Paris, 1673.

6. *Elias, The Prophet of Carmel*, P. Elias Magennis.

Spiritual Treatises:

1. *Pars Ascetica Regulae Johannis 44*, in *Analecta Ord. Carm.*, Vol. III.

2. *Les Oeuvres Spirituelles et Mystiques* of John a S. Samsone. Edition, Donatiani a S. Nicolao, Paris, 1658-59.

3. *De Ven. Johanne a S. Samsone, Insigni Mystico Ord. Carm., Johannes a S. Samsone, de Anima et Ingenio Ord. Carm.*, of John Brenninger in Analecta Ord. Carm., Vol. VII and Vol. VIII.

4. *Lettres Escriptes a son Pere Maistre en la Vie Spirituelle le B et St. F. Jan de Sainct Sampson* of Dominicus a S. Alberto, Tours Municipal Library, Codex, 488.

5. *Directoire des Novices ou Traite de la Conduite Spirituelle des Novices pour les Convents Reforme de l'Ordre de Notre-Dame du Mont Carmel* of Marcus a Nativitate, Paris, 1650.

6. *Introductio in Terram Carmeli et Gustatio Fructuum Illius* of Michael a S. Augustino, Brussels, 1659. Re-edited by P. Gabriel Wessels, Rome, 1926.

Historical:

1. *L'Ordre de Notre-Dame du Mont Carmel*, of Andre de Sainte Marie, C. D., Bruges, 1910. Translated into English, German and Dutch.

2. *Compendia della Storia dell'Ordine Carmelitano*, of Stanislao di S. Teresa, C. D., Florence, 1925.

3. *Historia Chronologica Priorum Generalium* of Ventimiglia, Rome, 1929.

4. *Speculum Carmelitanum et Vinea Carmeli*, of Daniel a S. Virgine Maria; Annales of I. Lezana; Bibliotheca Carmelitana of Cosmas a Villiers.

5. *The Scapular and Some Critics; The Sabbatine Privilege and The Scapular Devotion*, of P. Elias Magennis.